AN EMB

ALSO BY RICHARD GRIGG

Symbol and Empowerment:
Paul Tillich's Post-Theistic System (1985)

Theology as a Way of Thinking (1990)

When God Becomes Goddess:
The Transformation of American Religion (1995)

Imaginary Christs:
The Challenge of Christological Pluralism (2000)

To Re-Enchant the World:
A Philosophy of Unitarian Universalism (2004)

Gods After God:
An Introduction to Contemporary Radical Theologies (2006)

Beyond the God Delusion:
How Radical Theology Harmonizes Science and Religion (2008)

AN EMBARRASSMENT OF RICHES

AMERICAN RELIGIOUS PLURALISM AS A THREAT TO RELIGIOUS BELIEF

Richard Grigg

SACRED HEART UNIVERSITY PRESS
FAIRFIELD, CONNECTICUT
2012

Library of Congress Cataloging-in-Publication Data

Grigg, Richard, 1955-
    An embarrassment of riches : American religious pluralism as a threat to religious belief / Richard Grigg.
        p. cm.
    Includes bibliographical references   (p.   ) and index.
    ISBN 978-1-888112-29-0 (alk. paper)
1. United States–Religion. 2. Religious pluralism–United States.
 I. Title.
    BL2525.G75 2012
    201'.50973––dc23

                                                2012008259

For the students of Sacred Heart University,
who almost invariably show a genuine openness to the Other

Contents

Preface

The challenge to belief represented by the competing claims of the world religions has fascinated me for almost as long as I can recall. Indeed, it seems to me a challenge second only to the problem of theodicy for believers in God. Over twenty-five years ago, I concluded a book on Paul Tillich with an examination of how Tillich's thought might be developed into a "world theology," or what would today be called a "pluralist theology." I have taken the opportunity in this present book to consider the many different ways in which believers today approach the challenge of the potentially disconfirming Other, the member of a religious tradition different from one's own. It is not my intent here to propose my own solution to the challenge of religious pluralism, but rather to examine in depth the diverse strategies already on the scene, from outright denial of the problem to creative pluralist theological strategies to New Age agendas that essentially encourage seekers to abandon their traditional religious homes.

As with any book project, I owe much to many. Thanks to Debbie Alexander for her inspiration and for introducing me to various New Age practitioners and gatherings. Those introductions allowed for an empirical component in my examination of the New Age and its role in American religious pluralism.

My thanks, secondly, to regular conversation partners who never fail to provide the intellectual stimulation that I find is required to keep me going on any research project, even if our conversations are not always directly focused upon the project in question: Marla Ackerley, Christopher Sharrett, Walter Brooks, and Sidney Gottlieb.

Sidney Gottlieb must be singled out for a special word of thanks, for not only is Sid a model of scholarship, an expert on figures as diverse as George Herbert and Alfred Hitchcock, but he has served as the editor for this book, as for other Sacred Heart University Press volumes, and he carries out that task with extraordinary competence and artistry.

Thanks, too, to the referees who read the manuscript for the Sacred Heart University Press. I gleaned a great deal from their suggestions. It is obligatory to say – but in this case it also happens to be entirely true – that any weaknesses in the book are most likely the result of points at which I unwisely decided to disregard those readers' advice.

Finally, thanks to Dr. Seamus Carey, Dean of the College of Arts and Sciences at Sacred Heart University, who had an important role in seeing this project through to its completion.

Introduction

America has been the land of religious pluralism at least since the seventeenth century, when European nations began founding colonies in North America. There is no doubt that much light could be shed upon American history, as well as upon our contemporary situation in the United States, by contemplating how this religious pluralism has affected the whole sweep of our national experience. But what is at issue for us in the pages that follow is more narrowly philosophical and theological. In earlier eras, Americans were unlikely to encounter persons who embraced religions other than Christianity or Judaism. But today, we live in the proverbial global village. The explosion of new forms of electronic media makes it almost impossible for the reasonably curious American to avoid confronting religions other than his or her own. More concretely, the person occupying the office cubicle next to me may very well be a Hindu or a Muslim or a Buddhist. On an even more personal level, religiously mixed marriages provide a potent example of religious pluralism.

How does the diversity of other religions that the individual American believer must confront nearly every day undermine, whether explicitly or implicitly, the claims of his or her own spirituality? Philosopher Charles Taylor perceptively observes that this concrete confrontation of different belief systems results in their "mutual fragilization" and forces the individual believer to reckon with "the undermining sense that others think differently." The other believer threatens to become the disconfirming Other.[1]

Initially, America's spiritual and religious pluralism, far from appearing to be a threat to belief, seems wholly positive. First, this pluralism is a result of a robust spiritual culture: it is reasonable to suppose that we would not have so many spiritual options to choose from in America if there were not a large number of persons who wished to engage in the spiritual search. Pluralism is, in other words, a reflection of the fact that a significant number of Americans not only wish to be religious, but that their desire to be religious has led religious entrepreneurs to offer a host of religious options from which religious seekers can choose. Second, this pluralism is not only a result of spiritual robustness but actually has a causal role in reinforcing spirituality – more exactly, it reinforces the general phenomenon of the spiritual quest – because the very existence of so many endorsements of the spiritual quest lends that quest an enhanced plausibility.[2]

On the other hand, however, spiritual and religious pluralism confront the believer with a theoretical challenge. The specific options arrayed before me, as opposed to the general phenomenon of the spiritual quest, present competing spiritual worldviews that frequently contradict one another: Lutheran Christianity champions a God who graciously becomes a man in Jesus Christ in order to die on the cross to atone for human sin, while Sunni Islam holds that the very notion of God appearing in human form is tantamount to idolatry and that there is no need for a divine act of atonement. What is more, the all-important grounds upon which I assume that the claims of my own religious or spiritual worldview rest – divine revelation, for example, or supernatural intuition – are typically the very same grounds adduced by those pieties that contradict my own. Hence, I have no way to reassure myself, let alone the advocates of competing views, that my own claims are valid and that those that contradict them are invalid. Among a host of contradictory perspectives in which no one perspective is consistent with any of the others, one perspective, at most, can be sound. And because none of the perspectives possesses evidence by means of which to falsify the others, they effectively cancel one another out. Indeed, given that I hold to one spiritual worldview out of a whole menagerie of contradictory ones, the simple mathematical odds are that my own perspective is false. This is the potent challenge represented by Taylor's disconfirming Other.

We confront the paradox, then, that while the pluralism at issue here seems allied, by some measures, with spiritual fecundity in American society, it also possesses the potential powerfully to undermine belief. Thus it is that, although various commentators have opined for decades that a hitherto vigorous American piety might eventually succumb to the relentless onslaught of the scientific worldview or to some other force, we need to consider the possibility that the very success of so many spiritualities in America may actually prove to be a significant threat at least to the most parochial, unmodified forms of American spiritual belief. Where Christianity is concerned, which shall be our focus in this exploration, these traditional forms of belief are represented by "mainline" traditions, churches such as the Roman Catholic, United Methodist, Presbyterian, Lutheran, United Church of Christ, and Episcopalian.[3]

While terms such as "religion," "spirituality," and "pluralism" are hardly esoteric, the quest for precision dictates that we not take it for granted that their meaning is clear. I shall make an initial attempt to be precise here in the Introduction by offering an interpretation of the history of spiritual pluralism in America. This interpretation involves a decidedly brief rehearsal of that history, divided up into a consideration of the Colonial period, the roles of revivalism and fundamentalism, and the constant presence of what Catherine Albanese has called metaphysical religion.[4]

Religious pluralism was at the very heart of the Colonial experience in America. The Puritans, those English religious dissenters whose thinking was informed in large part by the theology of John Calvin and who established settlements such as the Plymouth Colony in Massachusetts, seem ordinarily to amass a disproportionate amount of attention in popular accounts of Colonial religion. They include, after all, the "Pilgrims" of grade-school lore, zealous god-fearers who made the famous journey on the Mayflower. But, of course, the Colonial experience was one of diverse colonies in no small measure because of the different religious groups that came to these shores: for example, significant numbers of Roman Catholics (among others) found their way to Maryland, Quakers to Pennsylvania, and Anglicans to colonies such as Virginia that were a function of entrepreneurship more than of escape from religious persecution. New York, which began as the Dutch colony of New Netherlands, illustrates all by itself the pluralism of the Colonial scene. As Winthrop Hudson and John Corrigan explain,

> When the English took over control of New Netherlands in 1664, the new colony was the most religiously heterogeneous area in America. The Dutch Reformed church quite understandably was the largest single religious group, and throughout the seventeenth century it was to continue to have more adherents than all other groups combined. But as Governor Dongan (a Roman Catholic) reported in 1687, there were also French Calvinists, German Lutherans, Congregationalists from New England, several varieties of Quakers, Mennonites, Baptists, some Roman Catholics, and a few Jews. "In short," he explained, "of all sorts of opinions there are some, and of the most part none at all."[5]

That is, the Governor is pointing out that, while many religious groups were represented in New York, the majority of his constituents had no strong opinions about religion.

Rhode Island, too, has a special place among the Colonies as a symbol of pluralism, insofar as Roger Williams was able to bring his convictions about religious freedom to fruition there, so that a host of different religious groups flourished. A small Jewish community could be found in Newport, Rhode Island, as early as the 1650s, and a synagogue constructed in 1763 can be found there still today.[6]

We are already in a position to catch a glimpse of the initial trajectory, at least, of American spiritual pluralism and to begin to make some terminological distinctions. We can take as our point of departure a statement that has become a mantra for a good many Americans today but that would have meant little or nothing to their Colonial forebears: "I'm spiritual but not religious." Ordinarily, one who makes this assertion means to suggest that he or she is interested in a life of participation in something beyond the contours of the visible world, a form of participation affording the experience of self-transcendence, but that such a life is not to be found within the confines of "institutional religion." That is, while "spirituality" is concerned with a quest for participation in a reality beyond the everyday and the resultant experience of self-transcendence, "religion" is here defined as a subset of that quest, one characterized by being part of a group with clearly defined rules of organization and requirements for belonging.[7]

Given this use of terms, what the brief survey above suggests is that Colonial spiritual pluralism was, on the surface at least, mostly of the "religious" variety: it was the result of institutionally well-defined groups, usually having an origin in Britain or on the Continent, rubbing shoulders in Colonial America. Even the Puritans, after all, though they were religious dissenters from the Church of England, were intent on establishing precise rules of membership and organization. And, despite their dissenting status, they owed the vast majority of what they believed to institutional forms of European Christianity that predated them. Similarly, while there was plenty of movement within early American Christianity, so that Congregational churches could end up being Unitarian or Universalist, for example, even Unitarianism and Universalism had European roots, and both took on recognizably institutional forms in this country. If "spirituality" is the broader term, then, embracing all forms of participation and self-transcendence in a reality perceived to be beyond the everyday, including the institutional subdivision called "religion," we can say that America has been spiritually pluralistic from the Colonial period on, but that in that period itself the pluralism was largely of the religious variety.

That it was not entirely religious in character, however, can be determined from two considerations, in particular. First, it is important to keep in mind that, despite the desire of some present-day commentators to present glowing accounts of a thoroughly pious early America, the Colonies had a significant number of inhabitants for whom God, religion, and spirituality were of little concern. While the fact that Colonial Americans were less pious than some would have us believe is not an example of religious pluralism, it nonetheless suggests more diversity than some would have us believe existed in early America. Recall the brief quotation from the Governor of the New York Colony cited above: while a whole host of religious opinions was represented in his colony, most inhabitants actually held to "none at all." Indeed, the available data indicates that church-going was at its lowest point in the whole of American history in the period from roughly 1750-1790, when only approximately seventeen percent of the population attended church.[8] Perhaps it is simply terminologically inaccurate to see the phenomenon of unbelief in Colonial America as part of its spiritual pluralism. Unbelief is not a form of religion or spirituality, after all, but rather its negation. But the element of unbelief does further variegate the spiritual scene in early America.

Second, and perhaps more important, many colonists were able to combine their adherence to a well-defined, institutionalized religious tradition with folk beliefs and practices that flourished outside institutional walls. Contemporary historians have gone to great lengths to show that the American colonists lived in a world full of heavenly portents and bizarre events in nature, of fearful acts of fate and uncanny evil forces. Colonists consulted fortunetellers and astrological charts and saw ghosts and monsters in the forests.[9] Thus, if it can rightly be said, as Shirley Jackson Case would have it, that the "sky hung low in the Ancient world," something very similar can be said for the atmosphere of early America.[10] As a result, we must conclude that early American pluralism was not only of the institutional religious variety – one might also dub this the "denominational" variety – but that it had wider spiritual dimensions.

Revivalism and fundamentalism added something distinctive to the American equation, and further enhanced spiritual pluralism on these shores. While revivalism as it developed in America had its roots in movements on the Continent and in Britain, such as

Pietism and Methodism, it took on a life of its own once transplanted here and insinuated itself into the fabric of American piety. One thinks, for instance, of the two Great Awakenings, of the eighteenth and nineteenth centuries respectively, and of their impact upon the American religious landscape. It is no accident that arguably the most paradigmatic of American composers, Charles Ives, drew much of the inspiration for his *Third Symphony* from the phenomenon of the camp meeting so much a part of American revivalism, nor that, on the other end of the musical spectrum, a seminal twentieth-century rock band, Creedence Clearwater Revival, took its name from the same phenomenon. Revivalism has had a lasting impact upon American culture.

One of the most significant features of early revivalism was its emphasis on individual religious experience. The believer expected to have what Søren Kierkegaard would call, however foreign the expression to the American believer's own ears, an "absolute relation to the Absolute."[11] Revivalism's emphasis on the individual and his or her proximity to the divine was paralleled in other varieties of American piety. New England Transcendentalism, for instance, whose preeminent representative was Ralph Waldo Emerson, had roots in the thought-world of intellectual luminaries such as F.H. Jacobi, G.W.F. Hegel, and Samuel Taylor Coleridge. But Transcendentalism's emphasis on the immediate presence of the divine to the human person ran parallel to the revivalist conviction that the believer ought to experience God directly, even though the latter had a less impressive philosophical foundation.

Fundamentalism is, at least in part, an offspring of revivalist Christianity. For while I have chosen to emphasize revivalism's emphasis upon the phenomenon of individual religious experience, such experience was, in revivalism, inextricably tied to a brand of preaching that was informed by a literalist reading of the Christian Bible. It was in the early part of the twentieth century that some Christians took the name "fundamentalist," holding firm to what they took to be "fundamentals" of Christian belief under siege in the modern world. These fundamentals included, above all else, a belief in the word-for-word inspiration of the Bible by God and the

consequent commitment to read it literally on everything from the
creation stories in Genesis to the account of the virginal conception
of Jesus in the Gospels of Matthew and Luke. Andrew Greeley and
Michael Hout describe American fundamentalism's origins this way:

> The movement which came to be called fundamentalism was
> born of the instinct that there could be no compromise with
> Darwinian evolution without the loss of Christian faith.
> Between 1915 and 1920 a group of conservative scholars
> published twelve short volumes called *The Fundamentals*,
> which laid down the nonnegotiable requirements of
> Christianity. In 1919 the conservatives founded the World's
> Christian Fundamentals Association (in opposition to the
> [mainline Protestant] Federal Council of Churches). . . .
> They charged that their adversaries were no longer Christians
> but founders of an entirely new religion.[12]

In more recent years, the term "fundamentalist" has probably
more often been used as a term of critique and derision than of self-
identification. Hence, while Christians who have accepted the
historical-critical approach to biblical interpretation initiated in
nineteenth-century Europe, can refer to their biblically literalist
counterparts as "fundamentalists," and while the press in the United
States frequently dubs militant Islamic groups as "Islamic
fundamentalists," today's Christian literalists are more apt to define
themselves with terms such as "evangelical" or "born-again."
Whatever the history of the term "fundamentalism," however, the
defensive theological posture to which it points is still an
extraordinarily important part of the pluralistic religious environment
in America. As a result, American spiritual pluralism is characterized
not simply by a cacophony of competing positive proposals for what
ought to be believed, but also by voices at least equally concerned
with the negative task of defeating, or at least holding out against,
forces seen as corrosive of genuine piety.

In addition to the large number of institutionalized forms of
belief – the religious denominations – that have powered American

religious pluralism and the dynamics that folk piety, revivalism, and fundamentalism have added to it, we must also consider the longstanding role played by what Catherine Albanese has dubbed "metaphysical" spirituality. In her magisterial history, *A Republic of Mind*, Albanese defines that all-important current of American piety by focusing on four characteristics. First, it is characterized by "a preoccupation with mind and its powers," where mind is an expansive concept ranging from cognition all the way to clairvoyance.[13] Second, metaphysical spirituality posits a correspondence between a divine macrocosm and the human microcosm (here the characteristic American emphasis on the proximity of the divine and the human, the emphasis on divine immanence, is in full flower) (p. 13). Third, metaphysical spirituality espouses an understanding of reality that emphasizes movement and energy (p. 13). And fourth, this characteristically American movement expresses "a yearning for salvation understood as solace, comfort, therapy, and healing" (p. 15). This metaphysical form of the spiritual quest includes everything from Theosophy to Christian Science, and it leads in our own time to so-called New Age spirituality and to discrete new religions such as Scientology. Of special importance for our purposes is the fact that this metaphysical piety contributes to American spiritual pluralism not just insofar as it is one more tendency to be added to the mix, but because, in Albanese's words, "the metaphysical world provides abundant materials that emphasize, especially clearly, its pluralism and, more, its fractiousness" (p. 7). That is, metaphysical spirituality is internally pluralistic; internal diversity is one of its most salient features, an especially relevant note that should be added, for our purposes, to the four defining characteristics of metaphysical piety listed above.

The dynamics of the forms of spirituality briefly considered here – Colonial piety, revivalism, fundamentalism, and metaphysical spirituality – continue to wield an influence in our own day. If Colonial pluralism was fueled first and foremost simply by the many different versions of institutional Christianity, along with a dash of Judaism, brought to America by settlers, the ongoing immigration so characteristic of the United States has continually added to our pluralism of religious institutions. Waves of immigration that brought increasing numbers of Jews, Catholics, Lutherans, Eastern Orthodox Christians, and other European groups to the United States have been followed by immigration from other lands that has added different world religions to the mix, including Hinduism, Buddhism, and Islam. As for revivalism, the emphasis on divine-human intimacy, far from being relegated to the period of the Great Awakenings, is today as American as cherry pie. For example, a significant number of contemporary Americans claim a "personal relationship" with Jesus Christ. And forms of Christian belief derived from fundamentalism often appear to be among the liveliest religious groups in America today. As already indicated, Albanese's metaphysical religion has a multitude of contemporary incarnations, most notably in the exceptionally variegated New Age movement.

But this extraordinary spiritual pluralism returns us to the most salient issue for our investigation: How does the individual practitioner's daily confrontation with the many potentially disconfirming others arrayed about her challenge her own spirituality? And how does the practitioner respond to that challenge?

Any consideration of the major challenges to belief in the modern and contemporary worlds necessarily entails mention of the much-debated phenomenon of secularization. Let us define secularization as it has most often been used by scholars, namely, as the process, beginning in Europe in the seventeenth century, in which the Christian religion gradually lost influence in Western society. While in the heyday of Christendom – that period during the Middle Ages in which the church had a potent influence over all dimensions of society – Christianity was simply inextricable from the larger culture, the modern period in the West has seen the church's authority, at least in many countries, retreating farther and farther into the individual or private sphere. With secularization, religion is no longer the primary authority in arenas in which it previously held sway. For instance, it no longer provides us with our primary descriptions of how the physical world functions – that task has been taken over by science – and it can no longer dictate how the economic component of society will be ordered. Religion, so the proponents of the notion of secularization aver, has been relegated to the private sphere. And even in the private sphere, religion and spirituality seem in some cases to be losing their power. Britain, Europe, and Scandinavia have all seen precipitous declines in both church membership and private expressions of piety.[14]

But what, exactly, lies behind the phenomenon of secularization? While it is naive to suppose that any mono-causal explanation could be adequate, one of the most frequently discussed potential causes is the rise of capitalism in the seventeenth and subsequent centuries, for capitalism's rationalizing dynamic empowered the economic sphere, allowing it to organize much of the rest of society around it. Religion, which had previously occupied that organizing center, was now pushed to the periphery.

However, secularization theory, as described above in terms of the rise to prominence of economic forces and the resultant privatization of religion, has become particularly controversial in recent years. That theory, in nearly all of its forms, assumes that institutional religion, and probably even what we have labeled spirituality, will continually weaken around the world as societies continue down the road whose starting point is modernity, and many proponents of the notion of secularization go on to assert that religion will eventually fade away completely. Yet, in sharp contrast to what the secularization hypothesis predicted, we seem to be witnessing the so-called "return of religion." From resurgent forms of Islam around the world to phenomena such as Hindu nationalism in India and the flourishing Pentecostal Protestantism in South America, religion and spirituality seem to be gaining strength rather than losing it.

But even if one interprets this present return of religion as just a temporary detour in the inevitable trajectory of secularization, one attributable perhaps to an unusual concatenation of socio-political forces that will not long endure, the spiritual situation in the United States has, for a much longer time, represented its own unique challenge to secularization theory. While it is true that the constitutional separation of church and state in this country is compatible with the privatization of religion often associated with secularization, it is impossible to miss the ongoing salience of religion in the lives of countless Americans. Nor should we overlook the fact that the principle of separation of church and state is constantly tested. Hence the challenge to secularization theory: If the process of secularization is an inevitable byproduct of capitalist rationalization, why is America so apparently non-secular? One might opine that, while capitalism is, according to the regnant theory, supposed to play a crucial role in religion's demise, capitalists may be ambivalent about religion, in that it can be a powerful tool for social and economic control. Certainly Karl Marx did not completely miss the mark in his analysis of how religion can function in a society.

But where the peculiar vitality of American religion is at issue, sociologists have frequently responded with a different explanation, one that draws on capitalist economics to suggest how America has avoided the capitalist economy's marginalization of religion and spirituality, but that does not focus on religion as a tool of control. Religion's startling vigor in the United States is, they aver, a matter of market forces and of competition in America. In Europe and Scandinavia, there has traditionally been an established church, such as the Anglican Church in England or the Lutheran church in Denmark. But insofar as an established church is protected from vigorous competition, propped up by taxes and tradition, it is likely to become fat and lazy, to atrophy for want of any vigorous commitment on the part of its constituents. But in the United States, with its constitutionally prescribed separation of church and state, there is no one protected religious species. And because no one spiritual group has an automatic leg up on the others, each group must compete with the others to stay alive. Each must aggressively market itself. Hence the long tradition of proselytizing in American Christianity, as well as among many new religious movements in this country. While the Jewish community, given its longstanding suspicion of attempting to make converts, remains a holdout in this regard – at least this is true of the mainstream American bodies of

Judaism, namely, Orthodox, Reform, and Conservative – such apparently unlikely candidates as the Unitarian Universalist Society have now enthusiastically entered the religious marketplace. One can actually find bumper stickers triumphantly declaring Unitarian Universalism the "Uncommon Denomination." In short, spiritual groups in America market themselves as aggressively as Ford markets Mustangs or General Mills markets Wheaties breakfast cereal.

If this analysis is sound, an analysis according to which American spiritual pluralism results in a marketing effort that keeps U.S. spirituality vigorous, then we must add it to the list of positive correlations between pluralism and piety, to be balanced off against our focus upon the potentially deleterious effects upon the most traditional forms of piety of confronting those who believe differently than oneself. It should be noted, however, that not all commentators accept the marketplace analysis as an explanation of America's apparently unique ability to withstand the forces of secularization. According to Gregory Paul, for instance, this explanation:

> owes much of its early acceptance to one of the greatest mathematical *faux pas* in the history of sociology. The statistical studies by Rodney Starke and Roger Finke that initially established the free-market competition theory of American religious vitality contained an egregious coding error: a key formula contained a -1 rather than the correct +1.[15]

He goes on to explain that

> Even before that extraordinary error was uncovered, Mark Chavez . . . and Philip S. Gorski had published a devastating 2001 meta-analysis of more than two dozen studies alleged to support the free-market hypothesis, concluding that "the claim that religious pluralism and religious participation are generally and positively associated . . . is not supported, and attempts to discredit countervailing evidence on methodological grounds must be rejected."[16]

We cannot say, for sure, then, whether it is in fact the free-market competition among religions in American society that has held off the full force of secularization on these shores. But whatever the role of market competition in particular in the perennial vigor of American piety, commentators will no doubt continue to cite that apparent vigor, whatever its cause, as evidence against the applicability of the secularization hypothesis to the American scene.

We should, however, bring a critical eye to bear on any credo according to which religion and spirituality have an absolutely secure place in American culture. After all, at the very center of our interest in this study is the notion that American spiritual pluralism may, in the long run, seriously undermine piety, or at least radically change it. The specter of the disconfirming Other is ever present. Hence, it may turn out that while American devotion has not succumbed to secularization – where secularization is understood in terms of the economy taking religion's place as the unifying center of the social order or, alternatively, as a weakening of religion due to other modern forces, such as natural science – that devotion will in fact eventually succumb to something else, namely, the individual's being forced concretely to confront a veritable chaos of spiritual perspectives other than his or her own, so that fatal seeds of doubt will be sown.

Now it will also be central to our thesis that the believer has a number of different options, some more intellectually honest than others, for responding to the challenge of the disconfirming Other. For instance, the believer can make strategic modifications to belief that may enable him or her to continue boldly to believe, modifications that defuse the Other's disconfirming power. We shall analyze this possibility in detail in Chapters Three and Four.

Still, it is certainly possible to find subtle signs of weakening in the structure of traditional American piety. That American piety might not be quite as secure as it initially appears, and that spiritual pluralism might be one factor undermining that piety, is plausible given a brief glance at recent empirical data. We must make it clear at the outset, however, that this empirical data provides scant evidence, if any, that it is pluralism in particular that is weakening

American spirituality. Rather, a glance at this data simply sets the stage for our discussion by showing that, whatever the causes, American spirituality is not without signs of being undermined. The "U.S. Religious Landscape Survey 2008" undertaken by the Pew Forum on Religion and Public Life looks to be the gold standard of religious surveys for some time to come.[17] While the study is voluminous, a few brief observations stand out, given our focus. First, the researchers found that

> More than one-quarter of American adults (28%) have left the faith in which they were raised in favor of another religion – or no religion at all. If change in affiliation from one type of Protestantism to another is included, roughly 44% of adults have either switched religious affiliation, moved from being unaffiliated with any religion to being affiliated with a particular faith, or dropped any connection to a specific religious tradition altogether.[18]

While all such changes in affiliation bespeak the pluralism of the American spiritual scene, the large number of unaffiliated Americans amidst this pluralism is consistent with, though by no means necessarily indicative of, the claim to be explored below, namely, that pluralism can tempt the erstwhile believer into spiritual indifference. Among those 18-29 years of age, one-in-four claim to be unaffiliated with any particular spiritual or religious group. The survey found that 16.1% of all Americans are unaffiliated. And while 5.8% of Americans consider themselves unaffiliated but still in some sense "religious," the remaining unaffiliated persons dub themselves wholly secular. Of particular interest is the fact that "those Americans who are unaffiliated with any particular religion have seen the greatest growth in numbers as a result of changes in affiliation."[19] Andrew Greeley and Michael Hout draw on other research to come to similar conclusions about the growing numbers of the religiously unaffiliated. They report that the number of adults who claim to have no religion doubled from seven to fourteen percent in approximately the last thirty years.[20]

A second indication that American spirituality might not be quite as healthy as it first appears is provided by the statistics on Roman Catholicism. While the number of Roman Catholics in America has stayed roughly steady over the past few decades, that turns out to be largely a function of foreign Catholics moving into the U.S. population. In fact, to return to the Pew study, "approximately one-third of the survey respondents who say they were raised Catholic [in America] no longer describe themselves as Catholic."[21] Pluralism might well be one salient factor here: immigrant Catholics tend to come from less pluralistic backgrounds, and first-generation immigrants tend to be shielded to some degree from the full force of American spiritual pluralism because they use their religious tradition as a tool for maintaining their identity, which is threatened by the sense of being strangers in a strange land. But a full third of American-born Catholics, those who do in fact grow up in direct confrontation with the disconfirming other, end up abandoning their Catholicism.

The Gallup organization's international polling only adds to the impression that, when compared to the spirituality of other lands, Muslim countries in particular, American piety is not as widely and enthusiastically embraced as an essential part of life as some might suppose:

> The importance of religion [in Muslim countries] is reinforced by what Muslims say about their traditions and customs, which also continue to play a central role in their lives. When asked, "Are there traditions and customs that are important to you, or not?" majorities in many predominantly Muslim countries say "yes": Jordan (96%), Saudi Arabia (95%), Turkey (90%), and Egypt (87%). This contrasts sharply with percentages of those [from a cross-section of persons from many religious traditions] answering "yes" to the same question in the United States (54%) and especially in European countries such as the United Kingdom (36%), France (20%), and Belgium (23%).[22]

Jon Meacham, writing in *Newsweek* and drawing upon the 2009 American Religious Identification Survey among other polls and surveys, offers some further sobering data in his provocatively titled article, "The Decline and Fall of Christian America."[23] He reports that "the percentage of self-identified Christians has fallen 10 percentage points since 1990, from 86 to 76 percent" (p. 34). In a *Newsweek* poll, 68% of the respondents said that religion is "losing influence in American society" (p. 36) What is more, "the percentage of Americans who think religion 'can answer all or most of today's problems' is now at a historic low of 48 percent" (p. 36). Perhaps most surprising, "the number of people willing to describe themselves as atheist or agnostic has increased about fourfold from 1990 to 2009, from 1 million to about 3.6 million. (That is about double the number of, say, Episcopalians in the United States)" (p. 34).

In his article "Is God Coming Or Going?" David Ramsay Steele, drawing in part upon the work of Pippa Norris and Ronald Inglehart on the relationship between religion and economic development, provides further evidence to bolster the claim that secularization is proceeding apace, not just in Europe but in the United States as well. Steele points out, for example, that responses to the Gallup organization's frequent polls on U.S. church attendance "exaggerate [how often the respondents actually attend church] by up to one hundred percent. We now know that U.S. church attendance has actually been falling steadily, and averages around twenty percent – higher in the South and Midwest, but lower in the rest of the country. U.S. church attendance is about four times that of the UK, yet still, church-going is distinctly a minority activity in today's America."[24]

There is another place to look for a subtle weakening of American spirituality in recent decades, despite appearances of its health. Popular culture in America has, in a span of roughly fifty years, gone from seeing "religion" as something essentially too sacred to treat with even a hint of irreverence (with undeniably important exceptions, such as the witticisms directed at religion by figures such as Mark Twain and H.L. Mencken) to a target ripe for ridicule. Think of Kurt Vonngegut's 1963 novel, *Cat's Cradle*, that makes fun of religion as essentially a clever scam designed to make our lives tolerable, all the way up to recent comic treatments of religion such as George Carlin's book *When Will Jesus Bring the Pork Chops?*, Lewis Black's *Me of Little Faith*, the antics of Jesus and his fellow world redeemers on television's *South Park*, and comic and social commentator Bill Maher's 2008 quasi-documentary *Religulous*. Black captures the mood of many of those tempted to skewer American piety: "I think [religion is] taken too seriously, and anything that takes itself too seriously is open to ridicule."[25] The kind of light-hearted approach to a topic that would, in an earlier era, have more often been treated with the utmost gravity, is illustrated by the following passage from Black's book:

> I feel [education is] more important than religion and, as it teaches the art of critical thinking, it can, under certain circumstances, even lead to religion. Religion, on the other hand, might lead you to education, but that usually only happens if you've been jailed and find Jesus and then Jesus says, "Hey stupid, get your GED, I can't understand you when you pray to me."[26]

What is more, there is no escaping the fact that religious pluralism is a crucial component of the religious dynamics that Black feels need to be skewered: "While it is true that many . . . religions think they are the only true religion, the one true way to God and eternal salvation, this is all . . . absolute bullshit."[27] While these quotations from Black are taken from one of his books, he mounts the same kind of offensive against institutional religion in America in his stand-up routines, some of them aired on such bastions of contemporary American television as HBO. While Lenny Bruce's criticisms of religion might have been as sharp as Black's, consider the utter implausibility of Bruce or any other comic back in the 1960s similarly skewering religion on the *Ed Sullivan Show* or the *Tonight Show*.

Film too tells us something about our now relatively relaxed attitude toward piety. The 1970s brought us *Oh God*, with George

Burns's genial and thoroughly innocuous deity, hardly the *tremendum*, the overpowering force traditionally associated with the God of Western theism. In the 1979, Americans happily imbibed a highly irreverent British import, Monty Python's *Life of Brian*, about a hapless and unwilling candidate for messiahship born next door to Jesus of Nazareth, a film that went so far as to find humor in crucifixion. Things became even more wildly impious in the 1999 film *Dogma*. While the Swedes can look back to classic Ingmar Bergman films such as *The Seventh Seal* (1957) and *Winter Light* (1962) for deadly-serious cinematic remonstrations of institutional religion, American (and British) filmmakers have become adept at comic treatments of a topic that would have been essentially off-limits before the 1960s.

In summary, then, an analysis of the state of religion and spirituality in the contemporary United States results in a mixed message. On the one hand, the number of different spiritual enterprises in America today seems well-nigh unlimited; spiritual pluralism could not be more in evidence. The multiplicity of pieties that surround us surely indicates that spirituality in America is far from moribund. But, on the other hand, both contemporary polling data and the irreverent attitude toward belief flouted in popular culture suggest that American religion and spirituality are also showing significant signs of strain, or that, though widely embraced, they are not taken nearly as seriously as they once were. In the chapters that follow, we shall interpret this mixed message as consistent with (but by no means exclusively caused by) spiritual pluralism's tendency to sow the seeds of its own undoing. Spiritual practitioners, sensing this threat, even if only subliminally, attempt to hold on to their beliefs through a number of different maneuvers, some of them merely defensive (we shall dub these "avoidance tactics") and some of them entailing creative changes in traditional belief systems (we shall call these "modification strategies"). It is these avoidance tactics and modification strategies that will take us to the heart of the matter. For while the juxtaposition that we have just undertaken of spiritual pluralism with empirical indicators of the weakening of traditional religious and spiritual allegiances is, at best, suggestive, the investigation of the avoidance tactics and modification strategies will provide a window into the internal logic of belief and pluralistic disconfirmation that our brief consideration of empirical data cannot accomplish. That is, the polling data adduced above, as well as the examples of treating religion less than seriously, by no means substantiate by themselves the thesis that pluralism can fragilize belief systems. There is little indication within that data that pluralism is the prime culprit in the weakening of belief. The point of our adducing empirical data, then, is simply to show that spirituality and religion and American do have chinks in their armor that must have been inflicted by various causes, of which pluralism might be one. Hence we must venture interpretive judgments that go beyond what the data we have adduced thus far has provided.

Yet logical argument will not be our only concern. For while our investigation is stimulated by a logical dilemma – "How can I assume that my beliefs are sound when I have no better grounds to embrace them than others have for their very different beliefs?" – our interest is in a whole host of ways that Americans respond to that dilemma. As a result, we will, in addition to more strictly logical matters, necessarily venture into the psychology of belief, especially when considering avoidance tactics.

CHAPTER ONE

Traditional Religion and the Disconfirming Other

Our investigation shall consider what responses are open to a traditional believer when met with the challenge of the disconfirming Other. But just who counts as a "traditional believer?" As with our stipulative definitions of religion and spirituality, we shall focus upon one particular type of believer in our investigation. He or she is the believer who does genuinely believe, that is, who does not underestimate the element of belief in religion and the truth claims that necessarily accompany what we call belief. This is obviously not to suppose that the cognitive dimension of spirituality is the only one that matters. It does not negate the importance of features such as ritual and ethical behavior; it does not treat these other components as mere epiphenomena.

Our "traditional believer," then, is a person who takes seriously the intellectual tenets of one of the great world religions and understands those tenets in a relatively orthodox manner. If we take a Christian as our example – since Christianity is by far the largest religion in America, it is Christians who will most often confront the problem of disconfirmation – this Christian is a someone who, at least before he or she is challenged by spiritual pluralism, is comfortable reciting the Apostle's Creed, for instance. Another way to express the matter is to say that our "ideal type" here is represented by the believer who has seriously entered into Anselm's laudable enterprise of "faith seeking understanding." Hence, our exemplary believer will be particularly alert to the problem of cognitive dissonance, that is, to points at which his or her religious beliefs seem to be contradicted by other plausible truth claims. Surely there are such believers. Indeed, if the intellectually astute believer described here does not in fact connect with any actual practitioners, then Christianity in particular, given its theological and doctrinal emphases, is in serious trouble. Of course, even these believers do not approach Christianity with a disinterested collection of philosophical abstractions about God. Although they are focused upon the cognitive dimensions of Christian beliefs, they connect the beliefs at issue here with their ultimate concern, and they are convinced that the deity whom they believe exists is to be unconditionally trusted, a way of relating to God that can appropriately be designated "faith."

But perhaps the whole project that I intend to undertake here – the examination of the different sorts of responses religious persons make to the realization that their beliefs are contradicted by the beliefs found in other religions – is fatally flawed because it places so much emphasis on having sufficient proof for one's beliefs. Aren't there many things that we believe that we cannot prove? As a matter of fact, we usually do not believe things unless we at least know how we could go about proving them, even if we do not have proof in hand at the moment. Suppose I tell you that I have loaned my good friend Frank a large sum of money, even though he would not tell me what he needed the money for. Do I have proof that Frank is trustworthy? Most likely, I do not possess indisputable proof, proof beyond any possibility of doubt. But I have the record of trustworthiness that Frank has displayed in all of his dealings with me up to this point. And if I really wanted to prove his trustworthiness, I could have him tracked by a private detective and find out what he intends to do with the money that I have lent him.

But this challenge, namely, that we ought not to expect the religious person to have proof for his or her beliefs, falters not only because we most often do in fact have something approaching proof for our beliefs – I might well take Frank's long record of trustworthiness as proof beyond a reasonable doubt – and because we know exactly how proof could be attained. It falters too because it trades on a false comparison. It compares beliefs we have for which we may not possess immediate ironclad proof with beliefs we hold that are confronted with strong evidence against them. The challenge of the disconfirming Other is about being faced with apparent disproof, and that is a significantly different situation from simply believing without incontrovertible proof.

However, the astute reader may offer another objection to the whole project that is at issue here. He or she may say that I am trading on just one notion of truth, a fairly narrowly scientific notion of truth. But aren't there many forms of truth? For example, doesn't an artful production of *Macbeth* communicate truth, at least to the most receptive members of its audience, and isn't that truth something other than the sort of truth associated with the natural sciences? We must answer both of these questions in the affirmative. But it is also important to note that religious belief, while it certainly appeals to various notions of truth, does have a large investment in something closely akin to scientific truth. For instance, belief that there is a supernatural consciousness that freely created the universe is a proposition, and it is closer in form to the claim that the Earth orbits the sun than it is to T.S. Eliot's poetic expression of the claim that modernity is a spiritual wasteland.

Having noted this kinship of religious truth claims with scientific ones, however, it is also important to note that we shall have occasion in our investigation to take other, non-scientific kinds of truth very seriously indeed. The modification strategies discussed in detail in Chapters Three and Four will certainly take us beyond any one, narrow definition of truth. For example, we shall take seriously Vietnamese Buddhist monk Thich Nhat Hahn's claim that the Christian notion of the Kingdom of God can in some sense be made consonant with the goal of the Buddhist spiritual quest, and this will require stretching the notion of truth beyond its narrowly scientific sense.

It is well to admit at the outset that the intellectually oriented, probing Christian lay person upon whom we are focusing is in the minority in most Christian churches. This is probably more the result of the larger culture in which American Christianity finds itself, a culture that has, not without reason, often been dubbed "anti-intellectual," than it is the result of any purely intra-Christian dynamic. The fact remains, however, that the problems that will be at the center of our investigation throughout this book may be consciously a problem for only a minority of believers. But to be simply unaware of the problem does not mean that the problem is of no consequence to the tradition in which one participates.

When the traditional believer is confronted with the disconfirming Other, modified versions of piety may emerge that serve to remove the apparent contradictions between his or her own convictions and those of the others encountered in America's heterogeneous spiritual landscape. Our exploration of such creative modifications and the strategies that produce them will be reserved, however, for Chapters Three and Four. At issue in this first chapter is what results from the confrontation with the disconfirming Other when one is not willing to go the distance required to produce a modified belief system that can remove the contradictions that pluralism brings to the fore. One opts instead for avoidance tactics. In Chapter Two, we shall analyze what might be deemed a half-way house between avoidance tactics and strategic modifications of belief, namely, fundamentalist belief.

In order to understand the relevance of modification strategies and avoidance tactics alike, we must first investigate just what can result from the believer's confrontation with the disconfirming Other. It turns out that there are at least three important results of this confrontation. First, it becomes apparent that the extraordinarily important concept of divine revelation cannot do the job that it is asked to do because, when confronted with the disconfirming Other, my conviction that something from my tradition is an instance of divine revelation is itself called into question. Second, the believer is forced into fideism. That is, he or she is forced to make a blind leap of faith and essentially to abandon the project of faith seeking understanding. And, third, the believer is left with a narrative about the relationship of the sacred and the profane that is characterized by a distinctive sort of bifurcation or fracture: whereas the profane is ordinarily parasitic on the sacred with which it is contrasted, now the profane seems to lose even this negative connection with the sacred.

Having considered these three results of the collision of one's beliefs with the very different beliefs of others, we will be in a position to move on to consider three avoidance reactions to the disconfirmation dilemma. These avoidance tactics should not be confused with the aforementioned strategic modifications to one's belief system: the latter attempt to alter one's beliefs so as to avoid disconfirmation, while the former are essentially attempts to evade the issue. The three avoidance tactics are the compartmentalization of one's worldview, the decision to see matters of religious belief as essentially immune to logic, and self-deception about the disconfirming implications of pluralism.

We begin, then, with the manner in which a robust pluralism renders the concept of divine revelation impotent, at least when the concept of revelation stands in its traditional, unmodified form. The great Abrahamic religions are all thoroughly tied up with the notion of revelation. Because God transcends the finite sphere in which we exist and to which our minds are proportioned, we can know very little about God, so the thinking goes, if we are left to our own devices. God is in heaven, and we are on earth. Any significant knowledge of God – whether of his ways or of the more specific details of what he expects of human beings – depends on God deigning to come down to humanity in order to show himself. The paradigmatic instance of this in the Jewish tradition is God's revelation of the Torah, his divine "teaching," to Moses on Mount Sinai. While the tablets of the Law provide the most tangible example of God's revelation, the Torah continues to unfold in the form of the oral law, the tradition of commentary upon which is enshrined in the texts known as the Mishnah and the Talmud.

Christianity inherits the Jewish concept of God revealing himself, and it takes up the idea of revelation in at least a threefold fashion. The ultimate revelation for Christians is the person of Jesus the Christ, God become man. But the Christ event is testified to in the New Testament which, along with the Hebrew Bible/Old Testament, thus becomes a source of divine revelation in its own right. And in Roman Catholic Christianity, the ongoing teaching tradition communicated through the leadership of the Church, the *Magisterium* (from the Latin for "teacher"), is a third source of divine revelation.

Islam, the third of the three Abrahamic traditions, offers what is perhaps the most straightforward theology of divine revelation: Allah has revealed himself via word-for-word dictation to the prophet Muhammad, a revelation mediated through an angel, recited by Muhammad upon its reception, and recorded in the Muslim scripture, the Quran.

But it is not only the Abrahamic traditions that depend upon the notion of divine revelation. The classic Hindu sacred text the *Baghavad Gita* (the "Song of God") contains revelatory insights provided by the god Krishna. The more philosophically dense collection known as the *Upanishads* does not in fact rest its claim to authority upon divine revelation, but, as we shall see below, the tradition that it was supernaturally intuited by special "seers" ends up raising some of the same difficulties in a spiritually plural world as do more straightforward claims to revelation.

As is so often the case, Buddhism seems to be the odd-tradition-out among the major religions. Because the Buddha has no apparent interest in the concept of a God, divine revelation is not on the Buddhist agenda. However, there are elements of the Mahayana branch of Buddhism in particular, such as stories of the Buddha wordlessly communicating a truth beyond ordinary concepts to a particularly adept disciple, that, as with the *Upanishads*, will end up confronting the Buddhist with some of the same difficulties that arise in other traditions when one faces the disconfirming Other.

Even if the implications of pluralism for the concept of divine revelation are seldom discussed in the theological literature, the concept of revelation is faced with a significant challenge, a challenge that might well be dubbed the Lockean paradox. The great eighteenth-century British philosopher John Locke recognized that, if it were unambiguously the case that I had access to divine revelation on some particular matter, I could rest assured that I possessed the greatest certainty imaginable on that topic. But here is the problem: "Our assurance can be no greater than our knowledge is, that it *is* a revelation from God."[1] The paradox, in other words, is that while divine revelation would always provide knowledge far superior and more secure than that available to finite, unaided human reason, human reason turns out to have the last word, for we must always make the human judgment that a particular claimant to revelatory status is in fact a revelation. Mere human reason always outruns claims to divine revelation; our own faculties necessarily stand in judgment over any and all alleged revelations.

Christian theologians, in particular, have been aware of this dilemma. That is why they have frequently maintained that the act of Christian faith, through which one accepts certain claims as revelatory, is not, in fact, simply a human achievement. Rather, Christian theology has often maintained that faith, and hence the acceptance of an alleged revelation as a revelation, is a gift empowered by God's grace. In the words of *Dei filius*, issued by the First Vatican Council in 1870, faith is "a *supernatural* virtue by which, *with the inspiration and help of God's grace*, we believe that what he has revealed is true."[2]

But this all comes to naught when the mainline Christian, for instance, confronts the many different spiritual options in his or her society. If I am such a Christian, why do I believe that Jesus of Nazareth is the incarnation of the second person of the divine Trinity? Because of revelation, of course. And I will add that my assurance that this is indeed a matter of divine revelation is provided not simply by my ability to produce reasonable arguments for its being so but through the illumination, the inner certainty, vouchsafed me by God's Holy Spirit. But here is the rub: When I confront my Muslim neighbor, I learn that she believes something very different about God and God's interaction with humanity. God is not triune, and God never did, and never could, become incarnate in a human being. The problem, of course, is that my Muslim acquaintance will claim to know this precisely on the basis of divine revelation, specifically, the revelation contained in the Holy Quran. It will do me little good to say, "But I know that my belief is the one based on genuine revelation, since I possess the certainty gifted to me by the Holy Spirit," for the Muslim will respond that her conviction that the Quran is divine revelation is equally certain, given that her conviction is not the products of her own reflection but, rather, is the work of Allah, all things being in His hands.

Claims to special faculties of knowledge, such as the examples provided above of the origin of the *Upanishads* or of wordless transmission of wisdom from the Buddha to a disciple, are in a precisely parallel situation to claims of divine revelation: persons from traditions different from my own will also claim to have special routes to knowledge, and the blatant contradictions between and among our competing claims will render the notion of special faculties of knowledge useless. When confronted with pluralism's disconfirming Other, claims to special spiritual ways of knowing are shown to have no more weight than claims to divine revelation.

In short, claims to divine revelation and its analogues, whatever their plausibility when set forth solely within the boundaries of single communities of belief, become impotent when confronted by other revelatory claims coming from other spiritual communities. There are simply no independent criteria, external to both Christianity and Islam, for example, that allow us to adjudicate between the competing Christian and Muslim claims. And if we add Hindus and Jews to the conversation, we will end up with a yet more cacophonous, and ultimately pointless, shouting match. There is an extraordinary reversal of fortune here, for, in one fell swoop, what initially appeared to be the paradigm of objective knowledge, namely, divine revelation, suddenly seems to be a function of mere subjectivity. It turns out that claims of divine revelation, so apparently essential to the content of theists' spiritual convictions, end up falling far short of their promise.

This fashion in which spiritual pluralism challenges the power of revelatory claims leads to the second result of the pluralistic confrontation mentioned above, namely, that the believer is reduced to fideism. The term "fideism," from the Latin for faith, is a kind of "faith-ism." It is the famous "blind leap of faith," an apparently willful decision to believe something when there is no rational evidence for the belief, but only the bare act of faith itself. There have been times in the history of Christianity, in particular, when fideism has been celebrated rather than condemned. But, ordinarily, these have been in settings in which the confrontation with other spiritual traditions was not in the offing; it was in these cases an intra-Christian dynamic at issue. In the nineteenth century, Søren Kierkegaard talked provocatively about faith as a "movement by virtue of the absurd."[3] He juxtaposed the absurdity of faith with the uncontroversial deliverances of reason in an attempt to call forth authentic Christian faith out of a Christianity that had become no more than a taken-for-granted cultural inheritance. Kierkegaard did not, in other words, retreat to a blind leap into absurdity as a response to the challenge of what Muslims or Hindus believed, but, rather, in response to a moribund culture-Christianity. Even Karl Barth, the great Swiss Calvinist theologian, despite the fact that he was a twentieth-century figure and thus already lived in a world aware of religious pluralism, set forth his fideistic theology within a decidedly parochial context. Barth was, once again, pitting his version of fideism against a form of Christianity, one that he believed put far too much confidence in the ability of our human faculties to grasp the divine.

It may well be the case that within the sort of intra-Christian conflicts fought by Kierkegaard and Barth, fideism can be shown to have certain advantages *as a spiritual practice*. But fideism surely proves useless when we step outside the confines of the Christian community and attempt to use it *as a theoretical tool to defend our beliefs when they are challenged by the disconfirming Other*. In the latter instance, as could have been anticipated from our discussion of the Lockean revelation paradox, the retreat to fideism can issue in little more than a shouting match among devotees of different spiritual perspectives.

The third result of the confrontation of unmodified mainline belief with the disconfirming Other is a special sort of bifurcation of the sacred and the profane. Students of religion have often noted how various cultures through time have divided the world into the sacred and the profane realms. The sacred, of course, is that dimension of reality infused with meaning derived from beyond the merely finite. It is the focus of the spiritual quest for participation and self-transcendence. The concept of the "profane" – the word comes from the Latin expression for "outside the doors of the temple" – helps to delimit the sacred; it is its counterpoint. But as with all binary concepts, it would be a misunderstanding to suppose that the sacred and the profane are somehow completely separate from one another, for they necessarily derive their meanings from one another. They are parasitic upon each other.

Although Plato's *Republic* is not ordinarily taken as a religious or spiritual document in the narrow senses of the term, this parasitism can be illustrated by his famous allegory of the cave. Plato contrasts the transcendent realm of the Forms, the ultimate source of what is, with the world of mere appearances in which we find ourselves here below. While he typically thinks in the abstractions of the philosopher rather than in the more emotionally-charged categories of the preacher, Plato's story provides a particularly clear metaphor for how the sacred or Real is related to the merely profane. The allegory of the cave depicts prisoners chained in a cave, facing its back wall. They are not allowed to see the figures that move back and forth in the outside world in front of the cave, but only the shadows that those figures cast on the wall. Our immediate experience of the world is analogous to the prisoners seeing mere shadows, for that immediate experience does not acquaint us with the Real, the Forms, but only with deficient imitations of those Forms. Hence, the Platonic allegory presents us with a division between the Real, knowledge of which requires something beyond our ordinary habits of perception, and the everyday world that we mistakenly suppose to be the Real. It is legitimate to equate this distinction with that of the sacred and the profane, not only in that that the Forms are transcendent, but also insofar as knowledge of the Forms and liberation from bondage to the merely apparent is necessary for our existential fulfillment or "salvation" as human beings.

What is particularly helpful for our purposes about Plato's allegory, as already suggested, is that it so clearly illustrates the manner in which the binary concepts of the sacred and the profane are not simple opposites but are parasitic upon one another. The images cast on the cave wall are indeed mere images, not the Real, but they are nonetheless images of what is in fact the Real. If the figures walking past the cave entrance were different, the shadows cast on the wall would be different too. One's particular notion of the sacred should dictate one's experience of the profane.

We can get a second view of this interdependence of sacred and profane by turning to what Mircea Eliade, probably the most famous expositor of the sacred-profane distinction, dubbed the *axis mundi*.[4] The *axis mundi* is literally the pole at the center of the world. Eliade's claim is that a vast number of spiritual traditions employ versions of *axis mundi* symbolism: they have images of a vertical structure that provides a passageway between the earth and the heavens, between the profane and the sacred. The Hebrew Bible story of Jacob's ladder, a ladder on which angels can move back and forth between heaven and earth, is one example. The Christian cross is an *axis mundi* symbol too, in that it is a pole – ancient Christian devotional language refers to it as the "tree," echoing the Tree of Life found in the Garden of Eden – on which Christ was crucified. The crucifixion purchases salvation, that is, access to heaven. That there are such passageways between the realms of the sacred and the profane illustrates once more that the sacred and profane are not traditionally conceived as simple opposites of one another such that never the twain shall meet. The profane is dependent upon the sacred, and what it means to live within the profane realm is determined by the nature of the sacred which stands over against it.

It turns out, then, that while the concept of the profane might initially suggest the mere absence of the sacred, the profane has ordinarily been a function of the sacred. And this means that different notions of the sacred should produce different notions of the profane. Note how dissimilar a pious American Methodist's perception of the profane normally is from the perception of an advocate of Iranian theocracy. The former will most likely perceive the distinction between sacred and profane as more pronounced than the latter. The Iranian theocrat does not deny that one can distinguish between the sort of relationship with Allah attained in the midst of prayer, on the one hand, and the implications of that relationship in a court of law, on the other hand. But to the extent that he or she maintains that the laws of the land should be a function of Shariah, that is, Muslim legal prescriptions derived directly from the Quran and Muslim tradition, the divide between sacred and profane will be seen as a smooth transition rather than an easily discernable break. The Muslim theocrat's expectation that the profane will reflect the sacred in a relatively direct fashion will be similar to the expectation of a citizen of Christendom in Europe's Middle Ages, where the Church could authoritatively pronounce even on economic matters, for instance, by prohibiting the charging of interest on loans.

But the seemingly logical expectation that the profane realm will possess distinctive characteristics based upon the distinctive perception of the sacred with which it is juxtaposed is confounded in pluralistic America. American pluralism resulted in the constitutional separation of church and state, which produced an unprecedentedly wide divide between sacred and profane. The width of that divide is only expanded by the highly rationalized structure of the American capitalist economy and its accompanying political and legal systems. This structure dictates how we shall behave in the profane realm, *regardless of our individual perceptions of the sacred*. Furthermore, the wide gap between the sacred and the profane created by the constitutional separation of church and state and its exacerbation by these additional structural features of our society is further increased as American pluralism is enhanced. If I am a twenty-first century American evangelical Christian, I must live in a society alongside Muslims, Jews, Buddhists, and New Agers, as well as with other Christians of a non-evangelical, liberal persuasion. The demands of practical interaction among all these different believers in the profane sphere, an interaction that demands that we all follow essentially the same rules of behavior, homogenizes the profane.

While different groups may still evaluate the profane differently – one sort of believer may attempt to be "in the world but not of it," while another sort will be perfectly comfortable in the profane world – the actual structure of the profane world will be largely the same for all. Of course, we ought not to underestimate the importance of these different evaluative judgments of the profane. This is, after all, in large measure, what the notorious "culture wars" of recent years have been all about. Evangelical Christians want the Ten Commandments posted in American courthouses, while members of more liberal religious or spiritual groups frequently do not. But the fact that such culture wars have taken on particular saliency in recent decades only testifies to the way in which the increasingly pluralistic character of American society pushes us closer to a homogenization of the profane, a homogenization that representatives of the "religious right" are convinced leaves out some essential beliefs and values. In the nineteenth century, hardly anyone interpreted the constitutional separation of church and state as dictating that it would be inappropriate to place a nativity scene, a Christian symbol, on the town green at Christmastime. Now that Muslims, Hindus, Buddhists, and Jews have a say in things that they did not have previously (not to mention the increasing significance of skeptical, non-religious voices), that nativity scene is regarded as unconstitutional. As pluralism continues apace, the profane's ability to reflect a particular brand of sacrality diminishes.

Let us return to the traditional notion of the sacred and the profane. As binary concepts, the sacred and the profane will always suggest a bifurcation: the profane is that dimension outside of the sacred, as the sacred is that which transcends, is of more value than, or is more real than the profane. But the bifurcation in the narrative of the sacred and the profane found in traditional societies, such as those discussed by Eliade, is a highly qualified bifurcation or fracture: the profane is indeed what the sacred is not, but it is nonetheless the particular sort of profane space that it is as a function of the particular sort of sacred that stands beyond it. What we have found in twenty-first century America, with its robust spiritual pluralism, is a different sort of bifurcation, a peculiar sort of fracture that separates the sacred and the profane. For now the profane is merely the non-sacred in an entirely general sense, rather than that which stands over against a specific image of sacrality.

A concrete example of this peculiar bifurcation is provided by the common morality we find in the profane sphere today. As the new breed of scientist-critics of religion, such as Richard Dawkins and Sam Harris, has pointed out, the moral standards actually practiced in American society (as well as in a sister society such as Britain), even by self-professed "Bible-believing Christians," does not really derive from the Christian Bible, at least not in any direct fashion.[5] Rather, even the fundamentalist Christian draws upon the common secular morality, what we can call here the morality of the largely homogeneous profane sphere.

Consider, as but one example, America's near-obsession with "family values" as the desideratum of our moral demeanor.[6] While it is true that one of the Ten Commandments orders us to "Honor thy father and thy mother," the larger set of family values so dear to evangelical Christians, values that are given lip service by the vast majority of Americans of all spiritual stripes, are not to be found in what is for Christians the most authoritative content of the Scriptures, namely, the teachings of Jesus. In one Gospel story, Jesus calls a man to be his disciple. Out of proper respect for his father, who has just died, the man asks to be allowed to bury his father first, before he travels away with Jesus. But Jesus will have none of it. "Let the dead bury their own dead" is his harsh reply (Matthew 8:22 and Luke 9:60). When Jesus is in a crowded room teaching and he is told that his mother and brothers are outside and wish to see him, Jesus dismissively replies that his real mother and brothers are those that follow him; blood takes a back seat to ideology (Matthew 19:46-50; Mark 3:31-35; Luke 8:19-21). Perhaps most dramatically of all, Jesus actually goes so far as to say that his followers ought to "hate" their mothers and fathers in comparison to their love for him (Luke 14:26). Try putting that version of family values on the Family Channel and getting a positive response from its targeted demographic!

There are innumerable spiritual communities available for us to join, but when it comes to our everyday behavior, our interactions with others in the profane sphere, our actions are less often a reflection of the vision of the sacred set forth in the spiritual community with which we identify, and more often part of a well-nigh common American value system, even if, as with all value systems, not all members of the society end up actually practicing what they acknowledge as the common ideal. The source of our moral values in contemporary American society is, in other words, one example of the way in which the profane sphere, the everyday world which persons of different spiritual persuasions occupy in common, is not a shadow cast by our idiosyncratic visions of the sacred. Instead the profane sphere is almost impervious to particular notions of the sacred.

We have considered three important results of the confrontation of mainline religion with the disconfirming Other, namely, the effective dissolution of the power of revelatory claims to back beliefs, the retreat into fideism, and an exaggerated bifurcation of the relationship of the sacred and the profane. This prepares us to move on to an exploration of three avoidance tactics employed by practitioners of traditional religion, responses that evade the challenge to modify one's beliefs so as to ward of pluralistic disconfirmation.

Of course, before we begin our investigation of these avoidance reactions, it must be acknowledged that some believers will not get even this far: not only will they refuse the opportunity to modify their beliefs in the face of the pluralistic challenge, they will not even engage in avoidance tactics. Instead, they will simply not confront the pluralistic challenge at all, perhaps because they have never thought through the implications of the fact that others' faiths have the same degree of evidential support as their own. The observation that there are undoubtedly some religious persons who are blissfully unaware of the challenge of the disconfirming Other, coupled with the fact that such persons are irrelevant to our whole investigation, forces us to recall the stipulation made above that we are dealing not with all believers, but with those who take the project of faith seeking understanding seriously. But, once again, those particular believers are not only a very real portion of the total population of believers, they are also the sorts of believers that religious traditions would most like to have.

Putting aside those traditional believers, then, who somehow avoid thinking about their neighbors' spiritual beliefs at all, we come upon three avoidance tactics employed in the face of the disconfirming Other. It is essential to be clear about what it is possible to claim about such tactics and what is beyond the reach of our investigation. It should be obvious that a philosophical analysis such as the one we are undertaking here, which does indeed draw upon the psychology of religion in addition to the philosophy of religion and theology, nonetheless cannot claim perfect access to the psyches of individual believers.

What is at issue for us, in any case, is a more theoretical undertaking: we begin with the uncontroversial fact that there are persons who hold what we are calling traditional beliefs, there being a host of traditional communities, from forms of Roman Catholicism and Lutheranism, for example, to equally traditional forms of Islam. We subsequently note that, if particular mainline beliefs go largely unmodified, they sometimes stand in stark contradiction to the beliefs held fast by members of other spiritual persuasions. For instance, Roman Catholic Christians hold that Jesus of Nazareth is the incarnation of the second person of the divine Trinity, while Sunni Muslims hold that the very notion of the Trinity is sacrilege, in that it compromises monotheism, and that the incarnation of the divine is equally unthinkable, in that it idolatrously reduces God or Allah to finite dimensions. We note, furthermore, that some Roman Catholics are quite aware of the contradiction between their own convictions and those of their Muslim fellow-citizens, and that they are equally aware of their inability to show that their beliefs rest on grounds that are more secure than the grounds upon which Muslim faith rests. We then take the straightforward step of looking for known, relatively uncontroversial psychological devices that can plausibly account for even an intellectually astute person's ability to live with such contradiction. The first avoidance tactic that we shall consider is compartmentalization, since it is in many ways the simplest of the three. Next we shall explore the self-conscious dismissal of logic in matters of spiritual belief. Finally, we shall investigate the tactic of self-deception, which can reasonably be regarded as the most psychologically complex of the three.

It is a truism, a chestnut of folk psychology, that human beings are able to compartmentalize what they believe. That is, they have the ability to hold both conviction "a" and conviction "b," even when "a" and "b" contradict one another, and they accomplish this feat by seeing to it that the contradictory convictions are never brought face to face. It is, in other words, as if there were separate compartments within the human psyche that, like the watertight compartments of a ship, can be safely sealed off from one another. Thus, I may firmly believe that Jesus of Nazareth is the incarnation of God but also recognize not only that Muslims handily reject this claim but also that I have absolutely no reason to suppose that my convictions are more securely founded than the Muslim counter-convictions. But I will compartmentalize the belief from the recognition, so that the two never confront one another.

As it turns out, we have a bit more to support the notion that human beings engage in compartmentalization than mere folk psychology. Contemporary neuroscience provides evidence that compartmentalization is indeed a common phenomenon. Rita Carter, who has written widely on contemporary brain research, shows in her book *Multiplicity* how the human brain switches back and forth between different ways of seeing and thinking when it encounters two contradictory possibilities so that it can embrace both of them. A concrete example is provided by certain visual "illusions." Take, for example, the line drawing, so often reproduced in psychology textbooks, that can be seen either as symmetrical facial profiles lined up nose to nose or as a vase. Most of us are also familiar with the figure that can be seen as either a duck or a rabbit. The salient point here is that our brains will allow us to interpret the figure in question in contradictory ways, *but that it cannot embrace those contrary ways of seeing at one and the same moment*: "your brain will allow you to see only one at a time . . . it just can't 'do' both patterns simultaneously."[7]

Carter goes on to explain that "this inability to see things in two ways simultaneously [but to see things in contradictory ways in sequence] occurs throughout the brain, including areas concerned with thoughts and emotions."[8] This suggests, of course, that the brain can and will hold contradictory ideas (not just contradictory visual interpretations) and that it will accomplish this feat by temporally compartmentalizing, that is, by focusing its attention on one idea at one time and on an opposing idea at another, without allowing the two ideas to come face to face in the same moment.[9] Spiritual pluralism can reasonably be read as one possible driver of this phenomenon. As Carter points out, "For most of us the options presented to us [in contemporary society] are increasing [including spiritual options] – life is getting more, not less, complicated. Hence, we switch from one way of seeing things to another, one way of being to another."[10]

That this temporal compartmentalization is indeed an avoidance tactic employed to deal with the disconfirming Other becomes all the more plausible when we factor in the role of emotion in some kinds of temporal compartmentalizing. Spiritual beliefs often entail a large emotional investment, given that they are about matters of ultimate importance to us: they deal with the meaning of life, the implications of death, and the moral principles by which we believe that we ought to live. One is understandably loath to give up beliefs that are of such extraordinary existential significance. Hence, if compartmentalization can prevent these beliefs from being undermined by a confrontation with the disconfirming Other, it is reasonable to suppose that compartmentalization will be an attractive option indeed. Consider an actual example. There are numerous Christians who disavow Darwinian evolution because they believe that it contradicts the Book of Genesis. Yet those same Christians take it as a given that pharmaceutical companies need continually to develop new antibiotics as bacteria become resistant to older antibiotics. Penicillin cannot cure all of the ills that it once could. Yet this phenomenon is nothing other than Darwinian natural selection.

The second avoidance tactic on our agenda is the self-conscious abandonment of logic in matters spiritual and religious. Let us return once more to our hypothetical mainline Christian, an intellectually responsible practitioner who has grown up reciting the Apostle's Creed on Sunday morning. At some point, however, the increasingly pluralistic character of American spirituality and the ever-more effective communication of that pluralism via new forms of media lead our believer to confront the challenge of the disconfirming Other: Hindus and Muslims and Buddhists, not to mention Jews and even some other Christians, do not believe what I believe, and I cannot produce any better evidence for my convictions than they have for theirs. My beliefs are crucial to who I am. They constitute, in Paul Tillich's familiar phrase, my ultimate concern.[11] Yet the chances of my beliefs being the one set of correct beliefs among the sea of competitors are mathematically slim.

The believer who is put in this apparently untenable position may well decide to take a page, as it were, from Job. While Job is concerned about theodicy rather than pluralism – though Job's so-called friends, with their conflicting views, might be said to represent pluralism – the answer that he receives from God may appear to be equally applicable to a contemporary person of faith facing the disconfirming Other. God famously makes the point to Job that divine matters are simply beyond human comprehension. Where were humans when God laid the foundations of the world? Faith too is, in the end, a divine matter, consisting as it does of a claim to be in relationship with God and to know certain things about God. Thus, perhaps I, taking the part of our hypothetical traditional and intellectually astute believer, will acknowledge that, on the one hand, I am certain about my faith convictions, while, on the other hand, I cannot intellectually solve the challenge represented by the other believer. But I may go on to conclude that this is where I simply ought to abandon logic, thereby releasing myself from the responsibility of explaining why my own convictions ought to be taken as more secure than those of other believers. After all, divine matters are beyond the grasp of human reason, and thus even the law of non-contradiction must sometimes be suspended when issues of faith are at stake.

It is worth noting that this willingness to abandon even the most basic canons of logical reasoning when it comes to matters spiritual is not without an impressive pedigree. The church father Tertullian is well known for glorying in believing in what appears to human reason as impossible. And centuries later, Martin Luther, never at a loss for the pithy phrase, referred to reason as the whore of the devil. If we desire a more contemporary example of the notion that, in matters of faith, logic does not always apply, we can look once more to the theology of Karl Barth.

This tactic of willfully transgressing the principles of logic may recall our earlier discussion of fideism, along with the incapacitation of revelation and the unprecedented disconnect between sacred and profane. But these were meant to be understood not as conscious tactics employed by a believer facing the disconfirming Other – that is what is at issue in the present case – but rather, as unavoidable logical implications of the dilemma of the disconfirming Other, the implications of which the believer might not even be conscious. One can take a blind leap of faith, after all, without ever reflecting upon the fact that it is blind. Hence, what separates our present discussion of the willful transgression of logic from our earlier discussion of fideism is that, despite the potential overlap between the two topics, we are thinking of the former as a self-conscious choice on the part of the believer.

The third avoidance strategy to be considered is self-deception. Georges Roy boldly claims that "Despite appearances, many Western adults who've been exposed to standard science and sincerely claim to believe in God are self-deceived; at some level they believe the claim is false."[12] Indeed, according to Roy, there are "reasons to suppose that anyone subjected to a standard Anglo-European high school education knows at some level that standard theistic claims are false."[13] If human beings can and do deceive themselves about the contradiction that Roy alleges between traditional theism and science – many would of course argue that no such contradiction exists – then it is to be presumed that they can also deceive themselves about the disconfirming implications of the Other's religious and spiritual convictions.

The notion of self-deception, however, is certainly one of the most puzzling concepts in all of psychology. How can one possibly deceive oneself? The concept implies that I know something to be true but, at the same time, succeed in convincing myself that it is not true. But that is a contradiction in terms. Yet, few would deny that most of us are, from time to time, subject to something that we would be willing to call self-deception. Scientist Michael Gazzaniga puts it in straightforward terms:

> We not only lie to each other, we lie to ourselves. From 100 percent of high school students who rank themselves as having a higher-than-average ability to get along with others (a mathematical impossibility) to 93 percent of college professors who rank themselves above average at their work, self-deception is at play.[14]

How can we make sense of the notion of self-deception, then? I suggest that in self-deception it is not the case that one is aware of the fact that what one believes (what one "knows" is true) is in fact false; that scenario is simply impossible to make sense of. Rather, in the case of self-deception, one recognizes that there is overwhelming evidence against what one believes. But given that belief is a matter of decision – I am not forced to believe in God, for instance, but decide to do so – there is no actual contradiction in my believing something even when I recognize that the evidence against that belief is overwhelming. The evidence that Frank is guilty of murder may be overwhelming, but the evidence may be misleading: Frank may in fact be innocent. The problem, however, is that if the only information to which I am privy is the overwhelming evidence of Frank's guilt and I have no good reason to believe that the evidence is misleading, my belief that Frank is innocent is an irrational belief. What is more, I know that the belief is irrational. This is, I think, what we mean by self-deception.

Human beings frequently engage in self-deception, understood in this fashion, in matters of health. There are numerous stories about persons who convince themselves that the rapidly growing mass that they are aware of in some part of their body is perfectly harmless, even when that mass grows to the size of a grapefruit. They convince themselves that the mass is harmless even though they are quite aware of the fact that, in the vast majority of cases, a mass of that size is not in fact harmless and should be surgically removed as soon as possible. They choose to believe something contrary to the evidence. There is no actual logical contradiction in doing so, but this is precisely what we mean by self-deception. I believe what I want to believe, knowing full well that the belief flies in the face of the available evidence.

My analysis of what is involved in the phenomenon of self-deception bears some resemblance, on two counts, to aspects of Freudian theory, though it by no means necessitates adopting the entirety of the Freudian notion of the psyche. First of all, self-deception as I have described it sounds, on some counts, like Freud's notion of wish fulfillment as laid out in his famous attack upon religion in *The Future of an Illusion*.[15] I convince myself that the mass growing in my abdomen is thoroughly benign simply because I so badly want it to be benign. Freud claims that this is what happens with belief in God: the believer has no evidence that God exists but so badly desires to tap the advantages that accrue to belief in a cosmic father figure that he or she convinces himself or herself that that cosmic figure actually exists. My description of self-deception is a bit different, however, in that it requires not that I believe in the face of the lack of evidence but, rather, that I believe *against* the extraordinary *preponderance of evidence* that I do know exists.

Second, the self-deceiver's ability to believe the opposite of what the evidence supports suggests a potent ability to avoid thinking about the evidence and its implications, and this ability might be seen as akin to the notion of Freudian repression into the unconscious (though it has no necessary connection to the whole Freudian philosophy of instinctual drives and traumatic memories that are supposedly forced into the unconscious, most often via strong social prohibitions).

Can this sort of self-deception be described as "lying to oneself," as Gazzaniga describes self-deception above? One might initially suppose that it cannot, given my rejection of the claim that self-deception is belief in something that one knows to be false. But Australian psychologist Dorothy Rowe echoes Gazzaniga's language while adding an account of the existential issues at stake that brings her understanding of self-deception into proximity to my discussion of that phenomenon, with its emphasis on what we wish to believe:

> We first experience the terror of being invalidated when we are small children, but by the time we are three or four we have learned a way of avoiding it: we have learned how to lie. From then on, whenever we glimpse the faintest possibility that our "selves" might be threatened with annihilation, we lie.
>
> First of all, we lie to ourselves. Why? Because we fear that we do not have the strength and courage to face the truth of our situation. We even lie about lying, preferring to call our lies anything but a lie. We say: "He's in denial."[16]

In any case, if self-deception as it has been described here is not only possible but common, then it is fair to assume that many persons go on believing what they have always believed in matters of religion even though they are aware of the evidence – in this case the simple fact – that the array of competing, equally-well supported, positions taken by their neighbors renders the truth of their own religious convictions mathematically unlikely.

CHAPTER TWO

I Believe Because They Don't: Fundamentalist Christianity

In the Introduction, we had occasion briefly to mention what is now ordinarily called "evangelical" or "born-again" Christianity, and we noted that the term "fundamentalist" is no longer the term that most conservative Protestant Christians use to designate themselves. However, I will use the term "fundamentalist" in this chapter to denote a defensive form of Christian belief, of which contemporary evangelicalism or born-again Christianity is one example. The term is useful, because it suggests the adherence to what are deemed fundamentals of belief that are under siege within the larger culture. The siege mentality is crucial for what I am calling fundamentalism here: Christian fundamentalism – and it is Christian fundamentalism rather than fundamentalisms of other varieties that I shall explore – can be designated an oppositional spiritual stance, one that is defined by the commitment to protect certain beliefs, deemed essential to Christian faith, from forces in the larger culture that are perceived as undermining those beliefs.

In the third edition of his classic study of American evangelicalism, *Mine Eyes Have Seen the Glory*, Randall Balmer effectively underlines the oppositional character of fundamentalist spirituality:

Ever since the 1925 Scopes Trial convinced fundamentalists that the broader American culture had turned hostile to their interests, fundamentalists have busied themselves devising various institutions to insulate themselves and their children from the depredations of the world. (In fact, the terms *worldly* and *worldliness* are probably the closest most evangelicals come to epithets; these words are often spoken sneeringly, in a tone at the same time condescending and cautionary).[1]

As a result of this oppositional stance, we encounter a "network of institutions – churches, denominations, Bible camps, colleges, seminaries, publishing houses, mission societies – that evangelicals built in earnest after 1925. The subculture made possible a wholesale retreat from the larger culture."[2]

Our particular interest in fundamentalism as an oppositional spirituality has to do with its relation to pluralism and the phenomenon of the disconfirming Other. Now the opposition that Christian fundamentalism has most vigorously mounted since its early-twentieth-century inception has been against such modern phenomena as the dictates of evolutionary biology and historical criticism of the Bible. But its oppositional stance has also included other religions. Most often, the other religions at issue have not been Asian traditions such as Hinduism and Buddhism (although its unrelenting foreign missionary activities are tantamount to opposition to these traditions) but, rather, the triumvirate of mainline or liberal Protestantism, Roman Catholicism, and Judaism. Mainline Protestants are seen as having abandoned crucial tenets of the faith. Roman Catholics have often been regarded by Protestant fundamentalists as hardly Christian at all, but as devotees of the merely human institution that is the Roman Catholic Church, which has usurped the role properly belonging to Jesus Christ, a Christ known not through the pronouncements of the Church but only in the Bible. As for the Jews, nothing could be much clearer than the pronouncement of a recent President of the Southern Baptist Convention (the single largest Protestant body in the United States and one of decidedly fundamentalist pedigree) that "God Almighty does not hear the prayer of a Jew."[3] Fundamentalist Christian organizations such as Jews for Jesus leave no doubt about the fact that, for fundamentalists, Judaism is deficient.

Nor should we overlook the fact that, even when we say that evolutionary biology and historical criticism of the Bible have been the leading incitements to fundamentalist defensiveness, we are still dealing with spiritual pluralism and its disconfirming Other: the larger American culture that has embraced science and historical criticism is not composed principally of atheists and avowed secularists, but, rather, of non-fundamentalist Christians and Jews who choose to integrate these modern ideas and methods into their own worldviews. Hence the aforementioned antipathy to liberal Protestants, Roman Catholics, and Jews.

When Andrew Greeley and Michael Hout lay out what they take to be the defining characteristics of "Conservative Christianity" in the United States, a concrete iteration of what I am calling Christian fundamentalism, they focus on three things: a literal reading of the Bible, an emphasis on the experience of being born-again, and a commitment to converting others to their version of faith in Jesus Christ.[4] The first of these, namely, biblical literalism, is at the heart of what I am calling fundamentalism, for one of the fundamentals that is perceived as being under attack in the modern and contemporary worlds is precisely the idea that God dictated the Bible word-for-word to its writers and that he intended it to be read literally. At first blush, the attack upon biblical literalism appears to come from the two quarters indicated above: the historical-critical approach to studying the Bible and the dictates of natural science, evolutionary biology in particular. The historical-critical method is largely a product of the nineteenth and twentieth centuries in Europe. To turn that method upon the Bible is to read it, not as dictation from God, but as the product of human beings living in particular times and affected by particular concerns and circumstances. As a result, the Bible is understood as a document motivated by forces parallel to those that motivated many other literary works from various locales in the ancient world. Natural science is seen by fundamentalists as undermining the literal inerrancy of the Bible insofar as disciplines such as geology, biology, and physics appear to contradict biblical stories about the creation of the world and humanity as well as biblical accounts of miracles.

But the sense of siege that fuels biblical literalism is tied to an additional phenomenon.

Though it is not as salient as historical criticism and natural science, we should not overlook the role of the pluralistic challenge in generating a tenacious, defensive biblical literalism among fundamentalists, for extra-Christian pluralism – the fact that there are many different religions – confronts the Christian with alternative scriptures, each claiming the sort of authority that Christians have usually supposed belongs to their Bible alone. Non-fundamentalist Christians might respond by embracing an interpretive freedom as the proper approach to the Bible (seeing much of it as metaphorical or symbolic, for example), which would theoretically allow them to avoid the conclusion that other scriptures contradict, and perhaps actually disconfirm, the Bible. In sharp contrast, the fundamentalist takes the oppositional tack of saying that the Bible must be taken wholly literally and thus should be regarded as falsifying any texts that contradict it.

Greeley and Hout's second defining characteristic, namely, the emphasis upon the experience of being born again, connects with our discussion in the Introduction of the importance in American spirituality generally of an experience of direct connection with the divine. The phrase "born again" itself comes from the third chapter of the Gospel of John in the Christian New Testament, where Jesus explains that, in order to enter the Kingdom of God, one must be born anew (John 3:3-8). That is, one must radically reorient one's priorities, away from selfish concerns and toward God and his Kingdom. There is a parallel message in another statement attributed to Jesus, namely, that one must lose the old self in order to find the new, regenerate self (Matthew 10:39). Christians of nearly all stripes would probably agree with this sentiment if taken broadly – indeed even spiritual traditions outside Christianity speak of the need for a radical reorientation of one's life, as in the Buddha's teaching about extinguishing the illusion of selfhood – but American Christian fundamentalists have given the expression "born again" a specific meaning. For the fundamentalist believer, to be born again is to have a powerful experience of the dissolution of one's old way of being and of having one's life reordered by being directly connected, via the act of faith, to Jesus Christ. The experience is sufficiently dramatic that fundamentalists often suppose that one should be able to name the precise date upon which the experience of Christian rebirth occurred.

The third factor that Greeley and Hout associate with what they call Conservative Christianity is particularly germane to our topic of pluralism: it is a hallmark of American Christian fundamentalism that its practitioners expend extraordinary effort to convert others to their viewpoint, to bring others to the born-again experience. The very phenomenon of proselytizing or evangelization is, of course, a function of pluralism. If one lived in a wholly homogeneous religious or spiritual environment, then there would be no need to convert others to one's own perspective, for there would be no other perspectives. But fundamentalists not only live among a host of other perspectives, they are characterized by a zeal for converting those who believe differently.

We shall return to this zeal to convert others as a response to spiritual pluralism. But first we must examine an even more basic move on the part of fundamentalism, one directed to all of the threats that fundamentalists perceive as arrayed before them, including pluralism and its threat of the disconfirming Other. As we have seen, fundamentalism is a spiritual worldview defined by a sense of siege. How might this siege mentality not only suggest the need for a defensive posture on the part of the fundamentalist *but simultaneously actually provide such a defense against the disconfirming potential of those who believe differently?*

We are, by now, familiar with the structure of pluralistic disconfirmation. I hold certain spiritual beliefs, and my grounds for those beliefs are claims of divine revelation or something akin to revelation. But I encounter persons with spiritual beliefs that contradict my own. By itself, this does not disconfirm my own convictions. The problem arises from the fact that those other persons make the same sorts of claims to revelation as grounding for their beliefs as the claims that I make. And this means that my belief system is, in effect, neutralized. We are faced with a host of conflicting claims and no reliable means for adjudicating among them and demonstrating that some of the claims are legitimate while their competitors are not. The contradictory spiritual beliefs cancel one another out.

Spiritual and religious beliefs – and here we are concerned with beliefs, as opposed to the many other phenomena associated with spirituality, such as engagement in ritual and the practice of prayer – are, of course, of a particular type. Unlike existentially neutral beliefs, such as my belief that Abraham Lincoln was the sixteenth rather than the seventeenth President of the United States, there is often a great deal riding on spiritual beliefs: both my sense of the meaning of life and my assumptions about the significance of death may well be a function of my spiritual beliefs. But there is another category of belief, one whose existential weight can be equal to that of spiritual beliefs, that is nonetheless distinct from them, namely, our moral convictions. One way to distinguish between the two is to note that, however important a spiritual belief is to me – for example, the belief that God exists – a spiritual belief is a conviction that something is the case. A moral belief, by contrast, is a conviction, not that something is the case, but that something ought to be the case: I ought, for instance, to love my neighbor as I love myself.

It turns out that the siege mentality in Christian fundamentalism introduces the special category of moral conviction into the mix in its confrontation with the disconfirming Other. This is of the utmost significance, because it suggests that, while I might find myself at an impasse if I had only my spiritual beliefs (and the grounding that goes with them) to put up against the disconfirming Other, the impasse can be broken if I have another sort of belief in addition to those spiritual beliefs, namely a moral belief. The fundamentalist concludes – and this is often one reason why he or she becomes a fundamentalist – that particular spiritual truths of the greatest importance are under attack and that it is therefore his or her *moral duty* to defend those truths. While the Other's spiritual beliefs might appear simply to cancel out my beliefs if my spiritual beliefs are taken just on their own, they do not in fact stand on their own. They are augmented by a distinct, additional category of belief, belief about my moral duties. Spiritual beliefs point to moral duties here because the perceived assault upon beliefs of ultimate importance makes it incumbent upon me to do all that I can to protect those ultimate convictions. And it is of the very nature of moral convictions that they are supposed to trump all else, to guide all aspects of our behavior, including our cognitive behavior. To take a non-spiritual example, my moral conviction that all people should be treated as equals will lead me to look askance at any cognitive claim that one racial group is mentally inferior to others, even if someone presents me with evidence for that cognitive claim that possesses initial plausibility. To the extent that the Christian fundamentalist experiences the disconfirming challenge of other belief traditions as an assault that he or she has the moral duty to repulse, the fundamentalist has potentially broken the impasse that results when one has only propositional beliefs (beliefs about what is the case) to put up against the propositional beliefs of others.

In order fully to understand the dynamic at work here, it is essential that we distinguish between a logical-argumentative analysis of this defensive move on the part of the fundamentalist and what we might call a phenomenological analysis. From a logical-argumentative perspective, the scenario that we have just sketched, in which the believer wards off the disconfirming assault of the Other via a sense of moral duty, is fallacious. One has a moral duty to defend certain spiritual propositions if and only if those propositions are true. But the very problem at hand is that the disconfirming Other puts me in a position where I cannot know that the spiritual propositions that I have been embracing up to this point are true. Indeed, if I consider the many different competing religious visions that exist in our pluralistic society, then the mathematical odds are against the spiritual propositions that I have hitherto embraced being true. From a logical point of view, then, the moral duty to defend the propositions, the card that supposedly trumps the cognitive challenge of the disconfirming Other, never actually arrives in my hand: if spiritual pluralism suggests that the propositions are most likely false, then the moral duty to defend them cannot arise in the first place. To put the matter in a slightly different way, the sense of moral duty arises too late.

Human nature being what it is, however, an analysis of the logic at issue will not necessarily suffice as an explanation of what actually happens when I confront the disconfirming Other. The designation of our species as *homo sapiens* is woefully incomplete if it is taken to mean that we will always follow the most logical course. In order to capture what, I wish to argue, frequently occurs in the fundamentalist's real-life response to the disconfirming Other, we must take what might be deemed a phenomenological approach. That is, we must ask, not what the rules of logical argumentation dictate, but what the fundamentalist believer experiences upon encountering the potentially disconfirming Other, what is actually given to his or her consciousness. This kind of phenomenological inquiry suggests, first of all, that the sense of moral duty will indeed appear as a "given," a dictum that confronts the believer as a powerful responsibility imposed on him or her from without and that, as such, has no chance of being interpreted as something that he or she is illicitly throwing into the gap. The analysis reveals, secondly, that the moral duty will by no means be experienced as something that comes too late, after the encounter with the disconfirming Other has destroyed the believer's truth claims and hence any moral duty to defend them. Rather, the believer will *experience* the moral duty to defend his or her convictions about ultimate truth as given *simultaneously* with the recognition that those convictions are under siege.[5]

The challenge of the spiritual Other, simply by threatening to undo one's own beliefs, rather than by advancing to the point of actually undoing them, already brings the moral duty to defend those beliefs to the forefront of consciousness. This phenomenological fact becomes evident not only in the zeal with which fundamentalists defend their beliefs but also the energy that they put into attempting to convert others. They go to the effort, in many cases, to walk from house to house and knock on doors, seeking to convince others to embrace their convictions, and many are willing to travel to far-away places to engage in this behavior.

Thus it is that the fundamentalist is defiantly averring, "I believe because they do not" and doing so in a twofold sense. First of all, what the fundamentalist picks out as the most fundamental of his or her beliefs – Jesus' virgin birth and the literal inerrancy of the Bible, for example – are a function of what is under attack by others. Secondly, his or her ability to hold onto the overall spiritual worldview that these fundamentals polemically symbolize is provided, in part, by the overwhelming sense of moral responsibility that arises precisely because of this attack.

Of course, the evangelical Christian form of fundamentalism, as is the case with other spiritual fundamentalisms, does not have to rely simply upon the believer's own resources to oppose the threat of the unbelieving Other. Many fundamentalist Christians passionately aver that God himself will go so far as to spirit the believer away from the potentially debilitating influence of that other. A sizable portion of contemporary Christian fundamentalists, true to the convictions of their forebears throughout Christian history, believe that Christ will shortly return to earth. Apocalyptic expectations, which include the expectation of the return of Christ, were apparently part of earliest Christianity, as is apparent from the Gospel of Mark, the first of the canonical Gospels to be written. While early Christian apocalypticism, which rises to a fever pitch in the book of Revelation in the New Testament, did not pay a great deal of attention to what contemporary fundamentalists call the "rapture," it is at the heart of much fundamentalist Christian piety today. Based on a short passage in Paul's First Thessalonians (4:17), the doctrine of the rapture, as it is most frequently articulated in the present day and age, holds that one of the first miraculous accompaniments of Christ's world-ending return will be the "rapturing" of true believers into heaven. That is, in one extraordinary moment, God will literally whisk the born-again away to heaven, leaving the unsaved on their own here below. If a true believer happens to be driving a car or piloting an airplane when the rapture occurs, woe be unto those left behind, who may find the now-unguided vehicle careening out of control and into their path. Hence the familiar automobile bumper sticker displayed by some fundamentalist Christians: "Warning: In Case of Rapture This Car Will Be Unmanned."

The implications of this rapture theology are genuinely striking. First of all, as already indicated, the clear implication is that the threat of the unbelieving Other will be supernaturally removed: born-again Christians will be taken up to the ultimate safe haven, and the potentially disconfirming Others will be left behind on earth. In fact, *Left Behind* is one title in the extraordinarily popular series of Christian apocalyptic fiction authored by Tim F. LeHaye and Jerry B. Jenkins, of which there is even a Hollywood film version.[6]

Second, not only will God take care of spiriting the believer away from the potentially corrupting influence of the unbelieving Other, but the theology of the rapture encourages the fundamentalist Christian to engage in undisguised *Schadenfreude* about the fate of that other. As their obvious delight in the image of out-of-control cars and airplanes wreaking havoc among the unsaved makes clear, devotees of rapture theology take solace in the notion that those whose beliefs contradict their own will be subject to a world of suffering precisely as a function of their holding the wrong beliefs. And the ante will be upped when the merely this-worldly suffering of the left behind is followed by eternal suffering in Hell when they die. As is the case with most apocalyptic thinking, going back to its origins in Judaism in the second century B.C.E. when Palestine was under the rule of Antiochus IV (the tyrant of Hanukkah fame), the threat to the faith is perceived as so great that it is necessary for God to step in and violently overthrow the present order. That so many Christian fundamentalists hold to apocalyptic theology as basic to their belief system – the imminent return of Christ is one of the beliefs listed in the all-important *The Fundamentals* mentioned in the Introduction as a founding document of Christian fundamentalism[7] – only serves to underline the oppositional structure of fundamentalism.

Having attempted to lay bare the basic oppositional structure of fundamentalist belief and one of the defensive moves that comes with it, it is now important for us to reiterate an important fact. While much of the sense of siege underlying fundamentalist Christian belief and the oppositional structure of that belief may have their roots in the historical-critical approach to the Bible and the dictates of the natural sciences (which is already an indirect encounter with pluralism, in that science and historical critique are embraced by other Christians and many Jews), a direct encounter with spiritual pluralism is also an important factor. I have already alluded to the incessant proselytizing activities of fundamentalist Christian groups, which includes both the attempt to convert various sorts of Jews and Christians to the fundamentalist fold and the desire to convert devotees of other world religions. We are all familiar with the overseas missionary work that fundamentalist Christians undertake in an effort to upend the spiritual convictions that animate non-Christian religions. But we do not have to consider simply what Christian missionaries are up to in places such as Africa and Asia to see the fundamentalist antipathy to non-Christian religions. At a rally for candidate John McCain during the 2008 U.S. presidential campaign, the former pastor of the Grace Evangelical Free Church in Davenport, Iowa, Arnold Conrad, offered up the following prayer:

> There are millions of people around this world praying to their god – whether it's Hindu, Buddha [*sic*], Allah – that his [Senator McCain's] opponent [Senator Barack Obama] wins, for a variety of reasons. And Lord, I pray that you will guard your own reputation, because they're going to think that their God is bigger than you, if that happens."[8]

To this list of opponents, we can add New Age piety, most forms of which are often seen by fundamentalists as anti-Christian paganism. As already indicated above with the example of the door-knocking for which fundamentalists are renowned – with Jehovah's Witnesses providing the clearest example – fundamentalist evangelization efforts occur here in the United States as well as abroad.

While the fundamentalist oppositional tactic explored above, which centers on the sense of moral responsibility to defend one's beliefs, can be applied equally well to the threat posed by spiritual pluralism in its most direct form, to the threat from historical criticism of the Bible, and to challenges from natural science, there is another fundamentalist strategy that appears tailor-made to address the threat represented by pluralism in particular: one can attempt to create one's own social plausibility structure.

Our beliefs will be the more firmly held the more inter-subjective validity they possess. In a society in which everyone believes that there is a God in heaven who rewards the righteous and punishes the wicked, the reality of that God can virtually be taken for granted. By contrast, if there are many persons in my midst who reject belief in such a God, the belief will seem to me, at the very least, open to question (the "fragilization" of which Charles Taylor speaks). In short, if my social group is characterized by unanimity in holding a particular conviction, it provides a potent structure for reinforcing the plausibility of that conviction.

The whole phenomenon of the disconfirming Other can be expressed in terms of the dissolution of any such strong social plausibility structure. Fundamentalist Christians, with their aforementioned predilection for constant proselytizing and for withdrawing into a self-generated subculture, are, in effect, creating a workable social plausibility structure: by converting others to their own religious worldview, they buttress their plausibility structure by increasing the number of persons who share their convictions; by retreating into a subculture, they maintain the integrity of a particular plausibility structure that might otherwise be undone by the presence of disconfirming Others.

While the zeal to convert others to their own belief system continues unabated within fundamentalist Christianity, the retreat into an independent subculture described in the quotations from Balmer above – the subtitle of Balmer's book is *A Journey into the Evangelical Subculture in America* – is not as thoroughly characteristic of Christian fundamentalism as it once was. Balmer himself is fully aware of a transition in this regard that actually began as early as the 1970s:

> . . . especially since the mid-1970s, as evangelicals began to
> emerge, albeit tentatively, from their self-imposed exile, . . .
> suspicion of "the world" has dissipated considerably. The
> antipathy toward the broader culture so characteristic of
> evangelicals in the twenties and thirties has gradually given
> way to ambivalence. Even as many evangelicals retain the
> old rhetoric of opposition to the world, they are eager to
> appropriate many of that world's standards of success. This
> explains, for instance, the proliferation of prosperity
> theology in evangelical circles.[9]

A particularly potent example of this so-called "prosperity
theology," which trumpets the notion that true believers, far from
needing to live abstemiously, should expect to receive economic
blessings from God, is provided by the extraordinary popularity of
preacher Joel Osteen. Today's fundamentalist Christians, including
those who tune into Osteen's television program and devour his
books – whether they identify themselves as born-again, as
evangelicals, or as fundamentalists – are perfectly comfortable
driving a new Mercedes and parking it in the three-car garage
attached to their mini-mansion in an upscale suburb.

But to say that fundamentalist Christians have emerged from
their previous cultural isolation insofar as they have embraced
contemporary American notions of success and wealth is not to
suggest that fundamentalism is no longer defined by an
oppositional mentality. On the contrary, precisely as a function of
their moving into the larger culture, fundamentalist Christianity has
spawned what commentators on American society have dubbed the
"religious right." That is, while they are now more than happy to
insinuate themselves into the larger social and political processes
(recall Jerry Falwell's Moral Majority and Pat Robertson's
presidential campaigns) that characterize American life,
fundamentalists energetically oppose much of what they see as the
norm in those processes. They vociferously oppose the Supreme
Court's *Roe vs. Wade* abortion decision, they agitate to bring prayer
into public school classrooms and the Ten Commandments into

courtrooms across the country, and they get out the vote to oppose legislation allowing gays to marry. Hence, the very notion of the "religious right" is defined by a sense of opposition on the part of its adherents toward what they take to be America's deficient mores.

Just as fundamentalists' emergence from an isolated subculture does not necessarily undercut the oppositional character of the fundamentalist mindset, so too it does not undo their attempt to create and reinforce a plausibility structure for their beliefs, thereby fighting back against the disconfirming power represented by pluralism. For one thing, the political activism that is part and parcel of the "religious right" phenomenon is, like the zealous efforts to convert members of other religions to fundamentalist Christian belief, an attempt to make the larger American society fall into step with the fundamentalist worldview, thereby creating a more effective social plausibility structure.

Given the continuing importance of shoring up the fundamentalist plausibility structure in the face of the disconfirming Other, especially as fundamentalists move out of their erstwhile cultural isolation, it should not be surprising that what is often dubbed the "mega-church" has appeared on the scene in contemporary American fundamentalism. For the mega-church allows fundamentalists to embrace important aspects of the larger culture while still wrapping themselves in a supportive plausibility structure. In essence, the mega-church sees to it that the church itself provides a broad array of services and activities that the believer has come to expect through his or her participation in the larger culture. It thereby allows one to buy into important currents of mainstream culture, but sees to it that those currents are monitored by a fundamentalist community. The mega-church is frequently a non-denominational, evangelical organization founded and led by a high-profile, communication-savvy preacher, a congregation with over a thousand members. But, once again, the mega-church is notable not simply for the number of its members, but also for the number of services and activities that it provides for them.

The stereotypical mega-church is built around a huge sanctuary boasting the latest in high-tech audio-visual equipment. That equipment will be augmented by a professional choir and band. One who attends such a church expects that the message proclaimed by its preachers, whose images will be projected on a huge viewing screen, will be reinforced by a spectacle as entertaining as anything that Hollywood has to offer. And what happens on Sunday morning is only a small portion of the story. The church may also have a bowling alley and a basketball court, along with organized leagues to exploit them, for church members to enjoy throughout the week. A church member who has a problem with substance abuse will not need to seek help outside the mega-church, since it will provide its own internal, Christ-centered support groups. Similarly, in a culture in which it is taken for granted that the problems that we confront are not a function simply of external challenges but are often problems best addressed through psychological therapy, the mega-church will have on its staff minister-therapists to offer its members the psychological support services that they require. In short, the member of a fundamentalist mega-church can have the best of both worlds: the believer can take advantage of many of the benefits that the larger, non-fundamentalist culture has to offer, but can enjoy those benefits within the safety of the church and its fundamentalist worldview. The plausibility structure for fundamentalist belief is thus kept intact even as American fundamentalism emerges from its erstwhile cultural ghetto. The disconfirming power of the Other is held at bay despite the fundamentalist's decision to buy into some of the perquisites of American culture at large.

Perhaps the best way to classify fundamentalism, then, when we consider its response to American spiritual pluralism, is as a halfway house between avoidance tactics and strategic modifications of belief. On the one hand, it is not a mere evasion of the pluralistic challenge.[10] Fundamentalism is a self-conscious and vigorous response to that challenge. But, on the other hand, its response is decidedly defensive in tone and attempts to hold onto certain "fundamentals" rather than to meet the pluralist challenge by strategically modifying belief in the fashion that we shall explore in the chapters that follow.[11]

CHAPTER THREE

Defusing Disconfirmation:
Modification Strategies

In the first two chapters, we have considered avoidance tactics and defensive reactions to the challenge represented by the disconfirming Other in a spiritually pluralistic America. But, of course, not all spiritual practitioners react to the challenge of pluralism negatively: there are also those whose response to the disconfirming Other is to see the disconfirmation at issue as essentially a positive provocation to rethink traditional forms of faith. They venture the possibility that, if they are willing to make some strategic modifications to the traditional faiths in which they were raised, it might be possible to remove the contradictions between one's own faith and that of others. The Other might then be no longer disconfirming but, rather, reinforcing, a fellow-traveler on the spiritual journey. While the New Age seekers profiled in Chapter Five also approach American spiritual pluralism positively, their strategy is almost *wholly to abandon mainline faiths,* those stalwart belief systems represented by American religious denominations from Catholicism to Methodism to Conservative Judaism. But the topic of this chapter is about how mainline religions might compromise. It is about letting go of some of the exclusivist claims of one's mainline tradition so that a core set of theological tenets from that same tradition can be harmonized with the convictions of believers from other traditions. While the main concern among those whom we discuss will be to find a degree of consonance among Christianity and other world religions, the principles set forth will have relevance too for harmony among non-Christian religions and spiritualities.

Anyone even remotely attuned to the violence that the clash of religions has generated around the world in recent decades, from India to Iraq to the destruction of the World Trade Center in New York City, must surely comprehend the urgent need for dialogue and understanding among different religious traditions. But such dialogue and the enhanced understanding that it aims to produce ordinarily do not rise to the level of the so-called modification strategies that we shall be considering in this chapter. In his book *Beyond Tolerance: Searching for Interfaith Understanding in America*, Gustav Niebuhr profiles a whole host of activists who seek, for example, "to find common ethical principles to bridge the volatile theological chasms" that separate traditions.[1] But the modification strategies that we shall investigate below seek not to leap over the theological chasms and onto the relatively safe ground of common ethical principles, but, rather, to descend into those chasms and do some serious theological prospecting. The modification strategies will grapple with the apparent contradictions in theological tenets rather than with the allegedly harmonious ethical outlooks of the world religions. While one representative of Jewish-Christian dialogue is quoted by Niebuhr as saying, "This isn't about meeting in the middle," the advocates of the modification strategies that will be at issue in our exploration often do attempt something sufficiently radical to be deemed an attempt to find theological middle ground.[2]

Our investigation will be divided into four main parts. First, we shall provide two brief examples of scholarly theological proposals that hold out the promise of defusing the disconfirming power of the Other via modification strategies. Second, we shall consider two other proposals, each seeking to show that the whole phenomenon of the disconfirming Other can be sidestepped as an illusion. In the third part of the chapter, we shall look at recent popular attempts to harmonize Christian belief with one or more other world religious traditions. Finally, we shall consider the argument that, while the modification strategies under discussion appear to avoid the problem of disconfirmation, they may in fact represent a particularly subtle variation on the theme of disconfirmation. That is, it may be that the modifications they make to traditional Christian claims about Jesus Christ give up too much: they actually disconfirm Christian belief by abandoning the "essence" of Christianity. This argument raises the possibility, in other words, that the modification strategies are simply one more example of pluralism fatally undermining belief.

Professional Theology and Modification Strategies

The twentieth century produced a vigorous discussion among academic theologians about how Christianity should approach the other great world religions. It has become commonplace in this discussion to distinguish among "exclusivists," "inclusivists," and "pluralists." The exclusivists maintain that Christianity is the one and only route to salvation. Inclusivists maintain that while all salvation comes through Jesus Christ, his salvific power is extended to non-Christians in some fashion. Pluralists attempt to see Christianity and other world religions as genuinely equal in the access that they provide to salvation, however that salvation may be conceived.[3] What we are terming modification strategies in our investigation belong in the pluralist camp. The pluralist approach is sometimes also called a "world theology" or a "theology of religions."

We shall begin by briefly examining the positions on Christianity and other religions set forth by two professional theologians in the twentieth century, the first inclusivist and the second pluralist.[4] We must begin our exploration of the two classic professional theological strategies with a crucial clarification: our focus in the whole of this study is upon the effect of the disconfirming Other upon the average believer, rather than upon professional theological discussion about the fact of religious and spiritual pluralism. Thus, the point of outlining the theological positions below will be to lay bear what they might, at least in theory, offer to those workaday believers. As a result, the real significance of the professional efforts profiled below is their potential to have an influence beyond the confines of academic theology. To what extent can they permeate, or have they already permeated, the larger cultural mindset?

Our example of inclusivism is provided by the German theologian Karl Rahner, often regarded as the single most influential Roman Catholic theologian of the twentieth century.[5] Rahner, who died in 1984, was a Thomist, a follower of the philosophy and theology of the greatest of the Medieval Christian thinkers, Thomas Aquinas. But he was a Thomist with a difference, a "transcendental Thomist."

Rahner reworked Thomistic theology with the help of Immanuel Kant's transcendental philosophy, which sought the conditions for the possibility of all our knowing, the preset configuration of the human mind that, as prior to any particular act of knowing, forms and limits our way of knowing. But while Kant concluded that the nature of the mind rendered knowledge of God, including the bare fact of God's existence, impossible (at least knowledge narrowly conceived, that is, "theoretical" or "scientific" knowledge), Rahner employed transcendental inquiry to a very different end: he argued that knowledge of God is not only possible, but that an implicit, subliminal awareness of God is precisely one of the preconditions of human consciousness uncovered by transcendental investigation. For Rahner, as for other thinkers dubbed transcendental Thomists, an inquiry into the preconditions for human knowing reveals the open-endedness of human consciousness, a trajectory that aims at infinite being.

Consider, first of all, the nature of human questioning. Asking questions is a crucial practice for our coming to know the world. But the human mind is set up in such a way that questioning never comes to a definitive end. The answers to our questions beget new questions. It appears that it is in principle impossible for us ever to come to an absolute end to our ability to ask questions. But this fact about the nature of our minds points, argues Rahner, precisely to the fact that those minds operate within an infinite horizon, the horizon of unlimited being, which for a Christian theologian is necessarily identified with the being of God.

Consider how, in parallel fashion, we use concepts to grasp reality, to know it. The medieval philosophers called concepts "universals," and for good reason: our concepts – dog, tree, goodness, distress – are by their very nature universal, in that they are universally applicable. That is, the concept dog – our concepts are, of course, tied to language and the words that help make up a language – can never be exhausted. Rather, it can be applied to as many dogs as might ever come to the attention of the human mind. Concepts are universal; they are open-ended. And this means that concepts, like the potential infinity of our questioning, reveal the open-endedness of all human inquiry, the fact that it is aimed at unlimited being.

This is not the same thing as claiming that we have a fully-formed innate idea of God implanted in our consciousness. First of all, the awareness of the unlimited horizon of being is not the same thing as the idea of a discrete infinite being, the Supreme Being of traditional Christian theology. Second, the awareness of the unlimited horizon of being uncovered by Rahner's transcendental analysis is, precisely as a horizon, not ordinarily the object of our attention. We do not consciously focus upon it. Rather, it is the context in which we think, the ever-present and encompassing setting, akin to what the ocean is for a whale. Hence, Rahner says that the constitution of our consciousness provides us with a "pre-grasp" or "fore-grasp" of the infinity of God. It is, as he also puts it, an "unthematic" awareness of the divine. This means that the infinite horizon is ordinarily not the conscious object of our reflection, yet we are subliminally aware of it. Of course, we can always turn to reflect upon this condition for the possibility of all thinking and awareness, making it a theme for consciousness as opposed to unthematic. And when we do so, we can, especially if we are schooled in Christian faith, then identity the presupposed horizon of conscisousness with the God to which that faith testifies.

Though Rahner himself is not interested in developing this line of thought so as to end up with a pluralist theology, one might see the *basis* for a pluralist theology here, that is, for a theological pluralism that interprets one's own faith as but one pathway to the same summit. After all, it follows from Rahner's analysis that all human beings have a real, if unthematic, awareness of infinite being. Might not the different world religions be simply different ways of understanding that self-same presence of the infinite, whether conceived as a substantive infinite or in terms of Buddhist or Taoist emptiness? Might not the differences between my faith and that of the Other turn out to be about relatively incidental matters of interpretation instead of about the heart of spirituality, which can here be interpreted as a deep and unavoidable connection with the ultimate reality? Might it not turn out, in other words, that the different beliefs held by the Other are not ultimately disconfirming of my own convictions, at least if I am indeed willing to employ a modification strategy that will allow me to regard certain features of my belief system as incidental to it?

Rahner's reason for stopping short of a radical pluralist position is not far to seek. He remains firmly rooted in the Christian tradition in maintaining Christ's unique, supernatural role in redeeming humanity from sin. All human beings do indeed possess, just *qua* their human way of being, an unthematic awareness of God. But each human being is also free and can use that freedom to place his or her individual being in opposition to the very God that provides the encompassing horizon for his or her existence. That is, I am always free to attempt to make myself my own god, to secure the meaning of my own being, turning my back on the encompassing presence of the real God, despite the fact that that encompassing presence is, at the end of the day, constitutive of my own true being. The reality of sin means that we are all, in fact, estranged from God and, thus, from ourselves. Some religious thinkers might imagine being extricated from such estrangement simply by coming to a fuller consciousness of God than the minimal, unthematic one with which we all begin, a goal that they imagine achievable via one's own spiritual efforts. Rahner, however, is a sufficiently orthodox thinker to depict the power of sin and estrangement in more dramatic terms and thus to require an equally more dramatic salvific role on the part of the Christ. Rahner does depart from some elements of traditional Western Christian thought by refusing to see the redemption effected by Jesus exclusively in terms of Jesus' atoning death on the cross. But by extending Jesus' salvific work to the whole of his existence, embracing his life as well as his death, Rahner only makes the unique work of the Christ all the more essential.

All of this means, of course, that, for Rahner, Jesus Christ cannot be seen as simply one clarifying lens, bringing the universal, unthematic consciousness of God more clearly into view, a lens that could have equally effective counterparts in the teaching of the Upanishads or the Buddha or the Quran. At the same time, Rahner does provide a fascinating version of inclusivism in his notion of the "anonymous Christian." For Rahner, one need not be in a dedicated and conscious faith-relationship with Jesus Christ in order to reap the benefits of Christ's saving work. Rather, someone who has never had the opportunity really to confront Christ may still attain salvation if that seeker does his or her utmost to respond to the gracious presence of God to consciousness that is the birthright of all human beings. But this person's salvation will nonetheless have been purchased by Jesus Christ, who effects the definitive, irrevocable victory of God over sin and estrangement. That the seeker in question may look to the Buddha as her spiritual guide while, unbeknownst to herself, she is actually put into proper relation to God via the saving grace of Christ means that she is a Christian despite her own self-understanding, an anonymous Christian. The anonymous Christian concept is an updating of earlier motifs in Catholic thought such as the so-called "baptism of desire."

Critics of Rahner inevitably point out that his concept of the anonymous Christian is condescending. Would a Christian, such as Rahner himself, want to be told that he is an anonymous Buddhist, only eking his way into a blessed spiritual state thanks to the work of the cosmic Buddha? Most likely not. But the problem of condescension is, of course, simply a manifestation of the fact that Rahner's position is a conservative, inclusivist instead of a radical, pluralist one.

Yet we ought not to dismiss this sort of inclusivism just yet, despite the fact that we are seeking modification strategies that can protect the believer from the disconfirming power of the Other in a fashion that does not sink to the level of mere avoidance tactics or amount merely to a defensive reaction. For while the potential disconfirmation most directly at issue in our investigation is the straightforwardly cognitive one to which we have repeatedly returned – the Other's beliefs, because I have no better grounding for my own, call my own beliefs radically into question – *there is also a non-cognitive type of disconfirmation that should not be overlooked at this point.* This less obvious threat of disconfirmation has to do with what we might term the disconfirmation of both the believer's own humanity and that of the other believer. Just to the degree that spiritualities and religions are often about what their adherents consider ultimate matters, those adherents may well fear that if the Other is wrong – i.e., in this scenario we have not yet gotten to the crisis of the cognitive disconfirmation of the adherent's own beliefs – that other may miss out on genuine fulfillment as a human being. And for some persons, a self-examination in which they find that they do indeed believe that persons with other faiths will forfeit the fullness of their humanity seems intolerable.

Indeed, just to find oneself holding this position about others may call into question one's own humanity: What kind of person can I be if I can consign my fellows to a status of less than full humanity (not to mention some version of an eternal hell after death)? But someone who adopts Rahner's anonymous Christian perspective will be freed of this burden. Disconfirmation of the believer's own humanity and that of those with other beliefs will be avoided. And this may be enough for some people. That is, as long as they can trust in the ultimate fulfillment of all persons of good will, they can rest easy in their faith.

Rahner is certainly not alone among contemporary Roman Catholic thinkers in offering this particular kind of solace, what we have called freedom from the disconfirmation of the other believer's humanity and of one's own. Indeed, no less a figure than the German theologian Joseph Ratzinger, who became Pope Benedict XVI, puts it eloquently:

> Everything we believe about God, and everything we know about man, prevents us from accepting that beyond the limits of the Church there is no more salvation . . . . We are no longer ready and able to think that our neighbor, who is a decent and respectable man and in many ways better than we, should be eternally damned simply because he is not a Catholic.[6]

Indeed, according to the Pope,

> The question we have to face is not that of whether other people can be saved and how. We are convinced that God is able to do this with or without our theories, with or without our perspicacity, and that we do not need to help him do it with our cogitations.[7]

Of course, at the end of the day, this solace about the Other's spiritual destiny, which is by no means insignificant, taken by itself does not confront the central challenge before us, namely, the cognitive disconfirmation threatened by the other believer. Yet, if we wish to designate this an avoidance technique, we ought nonetheless to recognize that it is an avoidance technique that deserves to be distinguished from the ones that we examined in Chapters One and Two.

There is another ramification of Rahner's position that takes us back to our main topic of cognitive disconfirmation, indeed that lets us deeper into some of the contradictions among the world's religions and, hence, the potential depth of the Other's disconfirming power. We tend to think of the disagreements between the faith of a Roman Catholic Christian, for example, and a Buddhist as about such relatively obvious topics as God and the afterlife. But some of those obvious matters, while literally of ultimate importance, are tied to some less obvious but absolutely basic assumptions about the human condition that, as such, are of hardly less momentous consequence. As our brief foray into Rahner's position has indicated, Rahner assumes, as any reasonably orthodox Christian theologian will, that humanity's greatest challenge is the problem of sin, which estranges us from God and, hence, from the very source of our own personhood. Thus, if religious faith is to provide us with anything, it must provide us with redemption from sin.

But numerous subdivisions of Buddhism begin with very different presuppositions. For the Buddha, and for much of the tradition that follows him, the dilemma in which human beings are ensnared is not sin, not some fundamental moral failure that blunts our potential humanity, but, rather, suffering. It was the famous passing sights of the haggard old man, the diseased man, and the corpse that set Siddhartha Gautama on his quest for Buddhahood. This only goes to show that the disconfirmation that the Other potentially wields threatens to sever not only the large and immediately evident branches of the tree of my faith, but even some of its roots, underlying assumptions so basic that I may scarcely be aware of holding them.

At the same time, the spiritual assumptions of American culture continue to change, and they do so at an ever-increasing rate. It does not take a great deal of imagination to suppose that one of the assumptions that many contemporary American Christians, even the most spiritually inclined, have left behind is that we are all ensconced in sin. Indeed, anyone who has spent time in a religious studies or theology classroom with the present generation of undergraduate students can testify that the burden of sin is not taken with anything approaching the seriousness that it once was. Whatever that change may mean for the health of traditional Christian theology, it is the sort of change that makes it significantly easier to meet the otherwise disconfirming Other halfway, for it will undermine the necessity of Jesus Christ being the (unique) atonement for sin. But the topic of atonement need not be left here: it will be appropriate to return to it at the end of the present chapter.

In order for professional theologians truly to meet the Other halfway, of course, will require that they offer a theological pluralist philosophy in place of an inclusivist one. The Anglican theologian

John Hick provides us with what may be the best known pluralistic theology.[8] And it is worthwhile to note the paradox that, while Rahner arrives at his rather conservative inclusivism through what many historians of theology would regard as a more "liberal" theological method, Hick comes to his pluralism via what has often been deemed a more "traditionalist" way of proceeding. Using the requisite theological jargon, we can say that Rahner does his theology, in large part, "from below," while Hick proceeds "from above." That is, Rahner opens up our initial approach to God not by citing alleged revelatory documents or special events of divine intervention (though these are clearly essential at later points in his theology) but, rather, by analyzing the supposedly universal nature of human being. He begins down here, with us. Hick, by contrast, will appeal to special divine acts of revelation that are alleged by the various world religious traditions themselves.

This is not to say that Hick does not use philosophical analysis and argumentation in order to prepare the ground for his pluralist theology. On the contrary, he makes a clever adaptation of that previously mentioned giant of modern Western philosophy, Immanuel Kant. Kant made a distinction between the noumenal world and the phenomenal world. The noumenal world is reality as it is just in itself. The phenomenal world is the world as we filter it through our noetic equipment, that is, the world as we perceive it. According to Kant, I never really know a cow as it is in itself, but only as it appears to me, synthesized by the forms and concepts that constitute my knowing process. Hick's claim, however, is that there is a special application for the noumenal-phenomenal distinction (one that Kant himself did not make) where God or the ultimate and its self-manifestations to us are concerned. Following the philosopher Karl Jaspers, Hick refers to an "Axial Period" in human history, beginning roughly with the Jewish prophets in the ninth century B.C.E. and continuing until roughly the fourth century B.C.E., in which relatively short time the roots of all of the great world religions can be found. Hick takes seriously the suggestion that this Axial Period represents the point in human history where human beings had become sufficiently sophisticated to receive special gifts of revelation. There is already a oneness, then, at the very birth of the world's great religions, including Hinduism, Buddhism, Judaism, Christianity, and Islam.

But what about all of the differences among those various belief systems? That, after all, is where our problem lies. Hick's proposed answer is that it is the self-same ultimate behind all of the revelations in the Axial Period. But that is, of course, the noumenal ultimate, the ultimate as it is in itself. And human beings have no access to that ultimate. Rather, the self-manifestations of the ultimate during the Axial Period must all be refracted through the lens not only of human cognitive capabilities generally but, more important here, through the very different lenses of diverse cultural milieus. Different cultures are different "worlds," after all: persons in different cultures actually experience reality differently. Hence, the revelatory light refracted through my cultural lens will inevitably look different from the light that beams through the lens of someone living in a different cultural world. Hence the payoff: I may see the ultimate in the form of the personal Supreme Being of traditional Christianity, while the person living to the left of me sees it in the Hindu Godhead named Brahman and the person living to the right of me sees it in the Buddhist Nothingness called Nirvana, but we are all seeing the same ultimate reality! The differences in what we see, which we might previously have taken to be mutually disconfirming, are not matters of contradiction at all; they are simply a function of the very same ultimate reality, in its noumenal aspect, having to traverse our different phenomenal filters.[8]

There are surely some attractive features in Hick's position for one who seeks a radical pluralistic theology. He seems to have succeeded in combining philosophical sophistication with an admirable cognitive humility. And, after all, humility is often taken to be one of the prerequisites for genuine piety. The spiritual quester who wants to hold onto the core of his or her traditional beliefs but who, in the humble recognition that his or her own cultural vantage point is necessarily limiting, is willing to make some compromises around the edges of those beliefs, would appear to have a useful ally in Hick. For instance, if a Christian can allow that the human need for redemption can be conceived in a number of different ways (though all involving relation to something ultimate) and that Jesus Christ is one of several diverse avenues to that redemption, cannot that Christian hold onto the essential core of his or her Christianity while now finding that the belief of others has lost its disconfirming power?

That is what Hick would like to have us believe, but his proposal leaves us with what some may take to be a significant unsolved problem. It is one thing to say that one person may see the divine in the form of a heavenly queen while another sees it in the form of a heavenly king. After all, the ultimate is not a physical being, so both kings and queens are simply metaphors in this case, and while the one metaphor might emphasize some characteristics of the ultimate while the other metaphor emphasizes different ones, there need be no contradiction in that. But the juxtaposition of the different belief systems represented by the great world religions presents us with much stickier instances than this.

For example, many Buddhists conceive of the ultimate not as any sort of being at all, not as any sort of God, but as incomprehensible Emptiness. Jews, Christians, and Muslims, by contrast, traditionally think of the ultimate as an all-powerful and loving personal being who created the world and who can intervene in their lives. Can one really say, as Hick must, that these are just two different phenomenal adumbrations of the same noumenal ultimate? The two different views appear to be not just different – different in ways that we can chalk up to interpretation or emphasis – but simply contradictory. And to claim that two contradictory claims are really just different interpretations of the same view might be taken to make the notion of "the same view" simply meaningless.

But whether this is in fact a fatal flaw in Hick's version of pluralist theology turns, in the end, upon one's assessment of his most central claim, namely, that the ultimate is so far beyond our phenomenal comprehension that we are faced not simply with each culture and religion falling short of anything like a full comprehension of the ultimate, but that that ultimate so transcends our grasp that even our logic is inadequate to it. If the latter is the case, then our notions of contradiction may simply not apply here, and Hick's position may be potentially sound. Critics, of course, will argue that to say that the ultimate transcends even the most basic principles of our logic is tantamount to saying that we really cannot understand anything about it all or make any meaningful statements about it.

It is also worth noting that, while Hick does employ Kantian philosophical notions, however highly modified, to advance his position, the overall weight of his proposal is largely a function of faith, and of empathy toward the Other. With his aforementioned theology "from above," Hick takes for granted the basic notion of revelation, which he sees breaking forth in particularly powerful fashion in the Axial Period. And surely a great deal of the convincing power of Hick's proposal, for those to whom it is in fact convincing, is a function not of complex arguments but of the ethical appeal of Hick's openness to the potential truth and value of all of the world's great religions.

In any case, while professional theologians will necessarily be concerned with the technical soundness of the arguments set forth by Hick and his fellow pluralists, what may be more important for the non-theologians is a certain permission granted them by the vigorous discussion of the equality of the world religions among the professionals. That is, to the extent that the spiritual quester sensitive to the beliefs of the others round about him is aware of theologians' work on radical pluralism, however ignorant of its technical details, that quester is freed to believe that his or her own path is but one avenue to the same spiritual summit. The non-specialist can feel justified in holding onto the core of his faith even though he neither possesses any evidence for his beliefs that the differently-believing Other lacks nor has worked out a technical modification strategy on his own. There are people who spend their professional lives thinking about these things, and they reassure the quester that there are perfectly consistent ways to see Jesus Christ and the Buddha as equally efficacious redeemers.

Isn't this, after all, at least one way in which shifts in the country's religious mindset often in fact occur, however glacially?[9] Professional theologians respond to new challenges that arise, precisely such as the challenge of a potentially disconfirming pluralism, and their own shifts in attitude in the face of these challenges eventually have an effect on large segments of the rest of the religious and spiritual spheres. Seminarians are assigned particular religious thinkers to read, and when those seminarians get to their parishes, the attitudes found in those works find their way into sermons and homilies. What is more, all perspectives can now reach the larger society more effectively than ever before, given the electromagnetic information bubble in which we are nearly all enclosed.

But, at the end of the day, it is almost by definition popular religious writers who have the most direct theological impact on American religious and spiritual attitudes. In short order, we shall examine three popular religious opinion-makers, thinkers who have a more direct effect upon Americans' sensibilities about the modification strategies that we might adopt in order to find an ultimate harmony among the world religions.

A Technical Aside: Does Belief Require Evidence?

Before we move on to our investigation of the popularizers of modification strategies, however, a technical aside is necessary: we need to consider an argument advanced by various Christian thinkers in the last part of the twentieth century that may seem to undercut the whole premise of the disconfirming Other. This argument suggests that religious belief cannot be contradicted by a disconfirming Other in the fashion that we have been suggesting it can. Our assumption has been that, if I have a spiritual belief system but I recognize that others have apparently contradictory ones, and I further realize that I have no stronger evidence than those others have for their beliefs, then that pluralism can be disconfirming of my own convictions. Indeed, if, with this dearth of special evidence, my belief system is only one of a large number of systems, and the systems are genuinely mutually contradictory, then the simple mathematical odds are that my belief system is wrong.

But what if the very assumption that, in order for my beliefs to be justified they require evidence, is in error? Wouldn't that mean that, even though I have no more evidence for my own beliefs than my neighbors have for their opposing convictions, that the whole challenge of disconfirmation would not arise in the first place? Justified belief, spiritual or otherwise, just would not be about evidence, at least not in all cases. Surely I hold some beliefs without any evidence, indeed without any grounding of any sort. For example, suppose that I believe that all packages of M & M chocolate candies contain more red candies than any other color, even though I have never bothered to count the color frequencies in even one package. For motives unknown to myself, I have simply come to believe that the reds predominate. This is an irrational belief, since it has nothing to back it up, but it is also trivial and, thus, most likely harmless. Other sorts of beliefs we hold had better not be irrational, though. If, for instance, a financial planner comes knocking on my door and asks to take over the management of my investments, I had better not just hand over my money. The belief that he or she could safely manage my assets without my having gathered any evidence to that effect would, like my beliefs about red M & Ms, be irrational, but this time my irrationality could have serious consequences. For my belief that the planner can in fact handle my assets safely to be rational, I would have to go to the effort of talking to other investors, looking for information about the financial planner on the internet, and so on. Thus, we have an example of a belief that has no evidence behind it and is clearly irrational and unfounded. And we have an example of a belief that could be rational if sufficient evidence were gathered before I formed it.

But might there be a third sort of belief, one that has not been formed via the accumulation of evidence but that is nonetheless still rational? Another way to put it might be to ask, "Can there be a sort of belief that I form without gathering evidence but that is still not groundless, and thus is still a legitimate belief for me to hold?" We get a positive answer to this question, specifically in the context of religious or spiritual belief, from Alvin Plantinga, a philosopher of religion who hails from the Reformed tradition and who concentrates on what he calls "basic beliefs."[10] These are beliefs that are not formed via the gathering of evidence but yet are not groundless, and hence not irrational. This seems to hold out the possibility that, even though I do not have any better *evidence* for my spiritual beliefs than someone with competing beliefs, that other believer need not be taken as disconfirming my beliefs, for evidence is not at issue.

The expression "basic belief" suggests a belief that is at the starting point of a set of beliefs. It is basic, so that it does not have to rely on evidence. Yet it is not arbitrary, as if I should just decide to make it a basic belief of mine that red M & Ms outnumber all other colors in every package of the candies. Plantinga gives as an example of a basic belief a so-called memory belief, namely, the belief that I had breakfast this morning. I believe that I had breakfast this morning. The belief is not based on evidence: I am sitting at my desk at work now, so I have no access to evidence in the form of dirty breakfast dishes in my sink, nor do I note any remnants of egg that I spilled on my tie. But to say that the belief does not rest on evidence is not to say that it is groundless: it is grounded in my memory of having had breakfast. Basic beliefs are a particular category of belief, then, that do not rest on evidence yet are not irrational. In fact, they are perfectly justified, and we employ them all of the time. Of course, as Plantinga points out with reference to his breakfast example, if I know that my memory is defective, then my belief that I had breakfast this morning could not in fact count as basic. I have to be unaware of any defects in my experiential equipment for the belief to count as properly basic.

Plantinga's intriguing move is to suggest that, for the genuinely pious person, spiritual or religious beliefs are often properly basic. I might believe, for example, that the God and Father of Jesus Christ loves me. There is nothing akin to ordinary evidence that I could amass to prove this to someone. But the particular contours of my life are such that I seem to experience the love of God for me in much that happens to me, parallel to how I have a memory of eating breakfast this morning. For me, then, though not for someone for whom my experience is unavailable, the belief that God loves me is a properly basic belief. It is not based on evidence that I could present in a court of law, but neither is it groundless or irrational. Once more, for me it is quite properly a basic belief. Thus, it would initially appear that even though my neighbor holds religious beliefs that contradict my own, and even though I cannot accumulate evidence to convince a jury of my peers – I cannot even collect *evidence* to convince myself – that my case trumps my neighbor's, my neighbor's beliefs are not disconfirming, for evidence is not required to confirm my belief in the first place.

The fatal difficulty here is that while Plantinga seems accurately to have described the notion of a basic belief and shown that such a belief is perfectly rational, religious or spiritual beliefs, the very ones at issue for him, lose their status as properly basic precisely when confronted with the contradictory beliefs of Others. My belief that I had breakfast this morning based on my memory of having had it is a properly basic belief, as long as I am unaware that my memory is defective. My belief would no longer be basic if my wife reported to me later in the day that, despite what I seemed to remember, I had been running late that morning and had skipped breakfast, and if my children confirmed her story. But notice what happens in my confrontation with the religious Other. I believe that the personal God of Christian faith loves me, and as long as nothing calls into question the life experiences giving rise to this belief, it is properly basic for me. But it is a crucial, defining characteristic of that belief itself that the "God" at issue is the Lord of the Universe, the Creator in whom *all* human beings move, live, and have their being. Now when my Buddhist neighbor reports that he has very different life experiences leading to very different basic beliefs, beliefs according to which all things are embraced in an encompassing Nothingness, my experiential equipment is called into question, just as when the efficacy of my memory is called into question, and my belief is no longer basic for me (nor is my neighbor's belief for him). In conclusion, the notion of properly basic belief will not serve as a modification strategy (nor even as a successful avoidance strategy, for that matter) to defuse the Other's disconfirming potential.

The Lutheran theologian George Lindbeck starts out from a different philosophical landscape but ends up in roughly similar territory to Plantinga's position, in that Lindbeck too calls into question the assumption that it even makes any sense for me argumentatively to defend my religious beliefs in the face of contradictory beliefs found in other religions.[11] Lindbeck thinks of a religion as a relatively self-contained "cultural-linguistic" world, not unlike the philosopher Ludwig Wittgenstein's notion of discrete "forms of life" with their accompanying unique "language games." It is not the case that Christians have religious experiences that form the particular language that they employ, but rather that their experiences are formed by the cultural-linguistic framework – in this case, the whole biblical story about life before God – in which they are trained. And just as the rules of baseball do not apply to the rules of basketball, and *vice-versa*, so the Christian and the Buddhist operate with beliefs and attitudes that are so independent of one another that there is no way to translate statements from one tradition in a way that will make sense in the other:

> When affirmations or ideas from categorically different religious or philosophical frameworks are introduced into a given religious outlook, they are either simply babbling or else, like mathematical formulas employed in a poetic text, they have vastly different functions and meanings than they had in their original settings.[12]

Hence, it once more appears as if we have come upon a perspective according to which the Other's religious beliefs cannot be disconfirming of my own. For my beliefs are part of the warp and woof of my cultural-linguistic world, and they will ultimately not make any sense when artificially transplanted into a different world.[13] Therefore, it seems that the very notion of contradiction between beliefs cannot arise here, for contradiction presupposes some common grammar of meaning upon which two assertions can rest.

But Lindbeck's position too falters. Note that persons within the Christian cultural-linguistic framework intend their statements about God to refer to a reality independent of any particular cultural-linguistic framework, including their own. Indeed, they will hold that the possibility of all such frameworks depends upon God's creation of human beings and his continual sustenance of them (even though this conviction itself will have to be articulated within the terms provided by their unique cultural-linguistic frame). And Lindbeck does not want to embrace the radical postmodernist position, something akin to a Nietzschean view, according to which there are no objective realities outside our frameworks and the different frameworks are simply alternative fictions. Hence, he floats the possibility that there is

> a sense in which truth as correspondence [with reality as it is in itself] can retain its significance even for a religion whose truth is primarily categorical rather than propositional [i.e., for a religion conceived as cultural-linguistic system]. A religion thought of as comparable to a cultural system, as a set of language games correlated with a form of life, may as a whole correspond or not correspond to what a theist calls God's being and will. As actually lived, a religion may be pictured as a single gigantic proposition. It is a true proposition to the extent that its objectivities are interiorized and exercised by groups and individuals in such a way as to conform them in some measure in the various dimensions of their existence to the ultimate reality and goodness that lies at the heart of things.[14]

It follows that it may be that

> there is only one religion which has the concepts and categories that enable it to refer to the religious object, i.e., to whatever is in fact more important than everything else in the universe [i.e., to what Christians call God]. This

religion would then be the only one in which any form of propositional . . . religious truth or falsity could be present. Other religions . . . would be neither true nor false. They would be religiously meaningless just as talk about light and heavy things is meaningless when one lacks the concept "weight."[15]

But now the problem of the disconfirming Other has simply returned in a slightly different guise, for I must recognize that many persons embrace religions different from my own, in other words, that those persons are ensconced in different cultural-linguistic religious frameworks. Yet, it is likely that only one of those frameworks, at most, can enable a way of life that corresponds to what is really the most important thing in the universe. And because we have no meta-perspective from which to compare the different cultural-linguistic frameworks with that most important reality as it is in itself, we have no way of determining which of the religions, if any, is the one framework that really does form a way of life that corresponds to that ultimate reality. The Other threatens disconfirmation of my beliefs after all.[16]

What have we discovered, then, in our brief detour from our exploration of modification strategies and onto the roads suggested by Plantinga and Lindbeck? Both thinkers put forth sophisticated proposals that may appear to suggest that, at least where religious belief is concerned, the problem of the disconfirming Other cannot arise. The very notion of disconfirmation, as we have laid it out, results from the believer's inability to present superior evidence for his or her own belief in the face of a contradictory belief. But Plantinga and Lindbeck hold out the hope either that evidence, superior or otherwise, is not required for my belief to be valid, or that the evidence that supports my beliefs exists within a discrete cultural-linguistic framework such that nothing arising from within a different framework can logically qualify as counter-evidence to my own. If these positions turned out to be valid, then we would, at the very least, have to radically rethink the idea that the Other can possess the power of disconfirmation. But, in fact, we have seen that, whatever their other merits, these positions fail to defuse the disconfirming power of the other believer.[17]

Three Contemporary Proposals by Popular Religious Writers

We begin with the Vietnamese Buddhist monk Thich Nhat Hanh (Thich is not a personal name, but a title bestowed upon Vietnamese Buddhist monks and nuns). Over twenty of his books have appeared in the United States, and he is a revered figure who had the chance to enter into dialogue with both Martin Luther King, Jr. and the Roman Catholic spiritual seeker and writer Thomas Merton. Many of his publications have been on the quest for peace, inner and outer. The particular work of concern to us here, however, is his book *Living Buddha, Living Christ*. It presents a pluralist approach to Christianity and Buddhism from the perspective of a learned and pious Buddhist. That Nhat Hanh is not afraid of a radical pluralism is apparent in a story with which he begins his book:

> Twenty years ago at a conference I attended of theologians and professors of religion, an Indian Christian friend told the assembly, "We are going to hear about the beauties of several traditions, but that does not mean that we are going to make a fruit salad." When it came my turn to speak, I said, "Fruit salad can be delicious! I shared the Eucharist with Father Daniel Berrigan, and our worship became possible because of the sufferings we Vietnamese and Americans shared over many years."[18]

Indeed, Nhat Hanh goes so far as to embrace the possibility that one can have more than one world religion as a personal spiritual root: his own experience has led him to graft Christian spirituality, as he understands it, as a second root onto the Buddhist root that has nurtured him throughout his life (pp. 99-100).

Traditional versions of Christianity have tended to see the risen Christ as the transcendent second person of the divine Trinity and to aver that God is in heaven while we are on earth, while Buddhists have been much more apt to look within to the possibility of personal enlightenment. It is safe to say, by way of initial summary, that Thich Nhat Hanh's approach to harmonizing Buddhism and Christianity is to put more emphasis than Christian orthodoxy upon the potential immanence of the divine in Christian faith. In this way, both Buddhism and Christianity can ultimately be about finding the ultimate within one's own individual experience. It is no accident that Nhat Hahn speaks more often about the Holy Spirit, which is usually associated with the immanent side of the Christian God, than with God the Father. Yet, this will turn out not to be an idiosyncrasy in Nhat Hahn's approach: in each of the writers whom we consider in this chapter, we shall see an ongoing focus upon an immanent God, in distinction to a God who is radically transcendent.

It should also be noted from the start that Nhat Hahn modifies the usual Buddhist interpretation of *anatman*, the doctrine of no-self. It would make little sense to talk about finding the divine within if there were no "within," nothing remotely resembling what we mean by selfhood. Siddhartha Gautama can certainly be interpreted as wholly rejecting the notion of selfhood, seeing it as an illusion, attachment to which leads to our suffering. But Nhat Hahn nuances his position from the Buddhist side in a way that will open up the possibility of genuine communication with Christianity:

> The Buddha did not present an absolute doctrine. His teaching of non-self was offered in the context of his time. It was an instrument for meditation. But many Buddhists since then have gotten caught by the idea of non-self. They confuse the means and the end, the raft and the shore, the finger pointing to the moon and the moon. There is something more important than non-self. It is the freedom from the notions of both self and non-self. (p. 54)

This means that there need be no contradiction between a religion such as Christianity, which clearly holds that we each have a core identity, a substantial selfhood, and the Buddha's attempt to get rid of views of the self that lead to suffering.

So too the Buddhist claim of the impermanence of all things should not be misinterpreted: "According to the teachings of Buddhism, it is important to look deeply into things and discover their nature of impermanence (*anitya*) and non-self (*anatman*). Impermanence and non-self are not negative. They are the doors that open to the true nature of reality," (183) in other words, to that which is in some sense beyond impermanence and illusion. They open to enlightenment, to the infinite or ultimate way of being that is often called Nirvana. And this is crucial for seeing the link between Buddhism and Christianity, for Nhat Hahn's claim will be that when the Christian looks within himself or herself, he or she will find the Holy Spirit and the Kingdom of God, that is, the ultimate beyond the impermanence and illusory character of the ordinary objects of our experience. What is more, this Kingdom of God is available in the here and now, not just in some distant heaven after death.

What the Buddhists call mindfulness is central to Thich Nhat Hahn's spirituality. In mindfulness meditation, one concentrates on the present moment. The many thoughts and emotions that constantly drift across the stage of my consciousness, thoughts and emotions that I ordinarily all-too-quickly identify with reality, including the reality of my own ego-self, are now observed as the ephemeral phenomena that they are. I am fully mindful of them simply as they appear in and of themselves, not as I am tempted to interpret and reify them. There is both a negative and a positive moment in this sort of meditational practice. On the negative side, my thoughts and emotions are emptied of their deceptive reality, and I am freed from the unhappiness and worry that often results from my emotional and cognitive attachment to them. On the positive side there appears an immediate experience of something that stands beyond these pretenders to reality, namely, the very observational perspective that is mindful of them. But what stands beyond the pretenders to reality if not genuine reality, if not what the Buddha meant by enlightenment and what Jesus meant by the Kingdom of God? Thus, experience, including the kind of experience at issue in mindfulness meditation, can provide an intuitive avenue to ultimate reality.

Thich Nhat Hanh's program for harmonizing Buddhist and Christian spirituality is furthered by his contention – it is not an unusual contention for a Buddhist, at the same time that it bears some resemblance to Hick's claims about the ultimate – that the ultimate is largely beyond our saying. The ultimate is beyond theology. "Discussing God," Nhat Hahn avers, "is not the best use of our energy. If we touch the Holy Spirit, we touch God not as a concept but as a living reality" (p. 21). Obviously, to steer as clear as possible of conceptual formulations and to focus instead upon experience helps to avoid disconfirmation. It is beliefs, after all, articulated in verbal formulations, that clash with one another and via which different believers cause the most trouble for one another. At the same time, we must be careful not to rush too quickly into the appealing arms of an alleged trans-conceptual religious experience. For philosophers have often pointed out that experience too requires concepts. For my experience to be an experience *of* something, for it to have any character as an experience, there must be interpretive categories in which it is formed, and that will require conceptuality. With this caveat noted, we can push a bit further into Thich Nhat Hahn's treatment of the underlying ultimate reality that he believes is opened to the quester by both the Buddha and the Christ.

It is a truism among contemporary New Testament scholars that the center of Jesus' message was the proclamation of the Kingdom of God. Of course, debates continue to unfold about just what he meant by the Kingdom. While Jesus may, according to one translation of Luke 17:20, have announced that in his ministry "the Kingdom of God is among you" (the rendering found in the New Revised Standard Version, the translation to which we refer throughout this book), there is also a familiar interpretation of that same verse according to which "the Kingdom of God is within you" (as in the King James translation), and it is the latter that best suits

Nhat Hahn's purposes. Of course, he adduces much more than that single verse to make his point. For example, he explains that

> Matthew described the Kingdom of God as being like a tiny mustard seed. It means that the seed of the Kingdom of God is within us. If we know how to plant that seed in the moist soil of our daily lives, it will grow and become a large bush on which many birds can take refuge. We do not have to die to arrive at the gates of Heaven. In fact, we have to be truly alive. The practice is to touch life deeply so that the Kingdom of God becomes a reality. This is not a matter of devotion. It is a matter of practice. The Kingdom of God is available here and now. Many passages in the Gospels support this view. We read in the Lord's Prayer that we do not *go* to the Kingdom of God, but the Kingdom of God comes to us: "Thy Kingdom come . . ." Jesus said, "I am the door." He describes himself as the door of salvation and everlasting life, the door to the Kingdom of God. Because God the Son is made of the energy of the Holy Spirit, He is the door for us to enter the Kingdom of God. (p. 38)

The ultimate is not a wholly other, radically distant reality. Indeed, the Christian Eucharist, in its own way, points us inward:

> The body of Christ is the body of God, the body of ultimate reality, the ground of all existence. We do not have to look anywhere else for it. It resides deep in our own being. The Eucharistic rite encourages us to be fully aware so that we can touch the body of reality in us. Bread and wine are not symbols. They contain the reality, just as we do. (p. 31)

Jesus' importance, then, is not principally as an extraordinary God-man who died on the cross to atone for human sin. Rather, he is a seer in whom God is powerfully present and whose teaching shows us how to find the presence of God, his Kingdom, within our own hearts. And, as Nhat Hahn points out above, this will not be a function so much of devotion to Jesus, of worship, but of following the practices that he teaches. And that, of course, sounds very Buddhist. The Buddha is not a being to be worshipped, but a teacher who shows the way to ultimate reality, to enlightenment.

At the same time, the Mahayana Buddhism that Nhat Hahn favors understands the Buddha, like Jesus, to be a teacher who is also the embodiment of the ultimate to which he points, an ultimate that one might go so far as to designate the "ground of being":

> After the Buddha passed away, the love and devotion to him became so great that the idea of Dharmakaya changed from the body of teaching to the glorious, eternal Buddha, who is always expounding the Dharma. According to Mahayana Buddhism, the Buddha is still alive, continuing to give Dharma talks. If you are attentive enough, you will be able to hear his teachings from the voice of a pebble, a leaf, or a cloud in the sky. The enduring Buddha has become the living Buddha, the Buddha of faith. This is very much like the Christ of faith, the living Christ. Protestant theologian Paul Tillich describes God as the ground of being. The Buddha is also sometimes described as the ground of being. (p. 51)

Especially if one can conceive the ultimate to which both the Buddha and Jesus point as essentially a matter of a higher form of experience that transcends theological categorization, then the Buddha and Jesus Christ do become strikingly similar figures here. "Christian contemplation includes the practice of resting in God," Nhat Hahn explains, which he goes so far as to say "is the equivalent of touching nirvana" (p. 154). Hence, "I do not think there is much difference between Christians and Buddhists. Most of the boundaries we have created between our traditions are artificial. Truth has no boundaries" (154).

At some points, Nhat Hahn is willing to leave the realm of esoteric experience and look for harmony amidst more conceptually constricted and apparently difficult differences between Buddhism and Christianity. He observes, for example, that "recent polls show that nearly one-fourth of all Europeans and North Americans believe in some form of reincarnation" (p. 131). And, he suggests, given the Christian belief that a soul must become incarnate in a body, the notion of reincarnation is not as inconsistent with Christianity as most Christian leaders through the ages would have us believe (p. 132). Finally, of course, the attitude that we have been outlining here makes it unsurprising that Thich Nhat Hahn is willing to see a degree of harmony not just between Christianity and Buddhism, but among all of the world's religions: "Only their manifestations are different. Authentic experience makes a religion a true religion. Religious experience is, above all, human experience. If religions are authentic, they contain the same elements of stability, joy, peace, understanding, and love" (p. 194). And yet, having said all of this – and despite his comment about fruit salad that we quoted at the outset – Thich Nhat Hahn does not look for some future amalgamation of religions. Rather, he expects that each individual can live happily in the religion of his or her birth, and live happily beside fellow-seekers in other traditions.

*   *   *   *   *

The second popular work that we shall examine is Deepak Chopra's *The Third Jesus.* Like Thich Nhat Hahn, Chopra is a prolific author. One might initially assume, however, that his many books and talks put him more in the category of a New Age therapist than that of a religious thinker, of however popular a bent, seeking unity among the world religions. But Chopra has a long interest in traditional Indian and Buddhist spirituality as well as the figure of Jesus. Indeed, he has written fictional accounts of the life of the Buddha and of Jesus. And we shall find that his argument in *The Third Jesus* overlaps with Thich Nhat Hahn's position in *Living Buddha, Living Christ* in instructive ways.

Given that Chopra himself is schooled in the Asian spiritual traditions, it should probably come as no surprise that his manner of harmonizing Jesus with Buddhism and various strands of Hinduism entails making Jesus more Buddha-like than making the Buddha more Jesus-like, at least where traditional understandings of Jesus and the Buddha are presupposed. Who, precisely, is the "third Jesus" of Chopra's title? The first Jesus is the actual historical figure Jesus of Nazareth, a man about whom we can never hope to know very much. The historical sources simply do not exist that would allow us to come to anything resembling a reasonably thorough biography of Jesus. The second Jesus is the Jesus Christ of the Church's ongoing theology, the Jesus of the creeds and theological tomes. For Chopra, as for numerous critics of Christianity at least since the nineteenth century, this second Jesus is almost wholly the Church's creation. But there is a third, real Jesus, or so Chopra, along with so many other questers, is convinced. Chopra, however, has a particularly provocative point of entry into his discussion of what he takes to be the real Jesus, for he claims that the problem with the first and second Jesuses is not just that they are essentially fictional, but that the frameworks provided by the first two readings of Jesus actually make Jesus' teachings impossible to follow. As a result, they appear to turn Jesus himself into a failure as a spiritual and moral guide.

It has been recognized since the inception of Christianity that dicta of Jesus such as "Love your enemies" (Luke 6:27) and "If anyone strikes you on the right cheek, turn the other also" (Matthew 5:39b) strain credulity regarding human moral capabilities. Various interpretations have been proposed. In the heyday of Christian monasticism, it was suggested that Jesus intended these most stringent of his teachings only for the monks. The teachings were known as the "evangelical counsels" and were not meant to be seriously imposed on lay Christians struggling to live in the difficult world outside the monastery. Some twentieth-century scholars proposed that Jesus' words represented an "interim ethic." That is, Jesus expected the imminent, literal end of the world, and while in ordinary life-circumstances one could not possibly maintain the rigorous standards he was proposing, a tiny community of believers huddled together who expected the end at any moment could in fact muster the ethical fortitude to respond, at least to one another, according to Jesus' dictates. But Chopra takes a different tack. What the Christian tradition has so consistently overlooked is that Jesus' moral teachings make sense only in the context of a wholly new iteration of human nature. Jesus had in mind a radical transformation of consciousness, one thoroughly foreign to our everyday perceptions of reality. That the transformation at issue is indeed a radical one is evident in the fact that the world we perceive via ordinary consciousness is essentially an illusion, akin to the Indian notion of the world as *maya*. At the heart of that illusion is the notion that the essence of each of us is something called the ego, a separate entity, a tightly bounded discrete self. Yet, even the most ordinary among us from time to time sense that our true being is something that transcends an ego-self:

> We are aware of beauty and truth. We feel led by intuitions and insights. In scattered moments we sense something beyond. None of these experiences is ego created. In fact, they are its enemy. Anything that gives a hint of life's wholeness, any experience that transcends "I, me, mine," threatens the ego's claim to dominance. This is because by definition, "I" is a separate entity. It wants certain things and not others. It wants to make friends out of some egos and enemies out of others. The one thing it can't abide is the reality that separate egos don't exist, that everything comes from a single source. Jesus brought just such a message to earth, and although he labeled it "God," in keeping with the language of his time, words aren't the same as experience.[19]

There is much here that sounds like the *Advaita Vedanta* tradition, the non-dual philosophy in Indian thought. And there is also much that sounds like what we heard in Thich Nhat Hahn's *Living Buddha, Living Christ*: the ultimate is an encompassing oneness beyond conceptual distinctions; this is the oneness that Jesus had in mind when he talked about God and about God's

Kingdom; it is a oneness that is to be attained in the here and now, not in the bye and bye of heaven; and this ultimate is something that we encounter via a particular kind of experience, with experience always a more accurate guide than theologizing. In Chopra's own preferred vocabulary, the experience of unity at issue here is tantamount to the attainment of "God-consciousness," and the more fully developed one's God-consciousness, then the more fully one has moved beyond the illusory world of the everyday.

Hence, for Chopra, "What made Jesus the Son of God was the fact that he had attained God-consciousness," indeed essentially a perfect God-consciousness, so that Jesus could say, "'the Father and I are one.' He knew no separation between his thoughts and God's thoughts" (p. 3). Now to claim that what made Jesus the Son of God was his perfect God-consciousness rather than his possessing a divine nature (along with a fully human one), as asserted by the Church's Council of Chalcedon in 451 C.E. or his being the one who could atone for human sin by dying on the cross, seems to add weight to the previously offered observation that Chopra's Jesus is cast in an Asian mode. Yet it is striking that to define Jesus' sonship to God in terms of his perfect God-consciousness echoes the Christology of the nineteenth-century German theologian Friedrich Schleiermacher, who is perennially tapped as the "father of modern Protestant theology."[20] And it should be unsurprising, given the common focus of Schleiermacher and Chopra, that both award special prominence to the Gospel of John, since its Jesus is indeed much more of an enlightened teacher, frequently discoursing on something akin to God-consciousness, than is the Jesus of the so-called "synoptic Gospels" (so named because they tend to "see together," i.e., to view Jesus in the same light), Matthew, Mark, and Luke. Thus, while we shall continue to note the Asian motifs that Chopra finds in his version of Jesus, we ought not to go too far in arguing that he is offering something terribly radical and unprecedented in his interpretation of Jesus.

According to Chopra, the real Jesus, then, sought to save humankind not by offering himself on the cross as a sacrifice for sin, but, rather, *intended to save the world by showing others the path to God-consciousness*" (p. 10; emphasis in original). Chopra admits that

Indians are scornful of outsiders coming in to skim the
cream of ancient Vedic teachings, turning yoga into a
weekend exercise class. Westerners are scornful of outsiders
coming in to claim Jesus as a teacher on the order of
Buddha and Muhammad instead of seeing him as the one
and only Son of God.

Once we move outside the boundaries of dogmatic
Catholicism and Hinduism, both positions can be seen to
have deep flaws. Consciousness is universal, and if there is
such a thing as God-consciousness, no one can be excluded
from it. By the same token, no one can lay exclusive claim,
either. If Jesus rose to the highest level of enlightenment,
why should he be unique in that regard? Buddha may be
his equal (hundreds of millions of followers believe so),
along with Vedic rishis like Vasishtha and Vyassa, who
didn't happen to have religions named after them. (p. 20)

Chopra's position clearly represents what we are calling a
pluralist theology, then, a modification strategy that seeks to allow
a hypothetical Christian to acknowledge the Other's beliefs – with
the Other in this case being a Buddhist or Hindu – without those
beliefs necessarily proving disconfirming to what that Christian
regards as the essential core of his or her own belief system.[21] Of
course, a crucial component in the success or failure of such a
modification strategy will be the Christian's decision about just
what does constitute the nonnegotiable, essential heart of her faith.
We shall return to the concept of the "essence" of Christianity later
in this chapter.

What is most distinctive about Chopra's pluralist theology is the
previously noted emphasis on our ordinary consciousness as illusory.
In the everyday mode of consciousness, it is genuinely impossible to
follow Jesus' most stringent commands, such as returning love for
hate or refusing to resist evil. But in the transformed mode that
Chopra calls God-consciousness, the impossible becomes possible:
"to the extent that you rise toward God-consciousness, evil
withdraws, leaving you invulnerable" (p. 27).

"Evil is everything when you are susceptible to it; it is nothing when you aren't" Chopra avers (p. 27). If Jesus was not quite as explicit about how this all works as we might like, Chopra thinks that we can fill in some of the blanks by drawing upon the world's various wisdom traditions. For example, consider what those traditions teach about meditation:

> Sit every day and find the silence insider yourself. In this silence, there is peace without anger. There is no evil, no attachment to revenge or righteous indignation. With practice, you learn to identify yourself with this place. It becomes natural to master anger, an energy like any other. When this happens, evil begins to release you from its hold. (p. 27)

Again,

> When you fear evil, you are certain that it must be real. This certainty forces you to engage in the eternal struggle between good and evil. No amount of passive resistance will extricate you . . . . But if you can see that the war between good and evil is nothing but a play of light and shadow, your certainty about the existence of evil will fade away. (p. 28)

Chopra goes so far as to assert that

> despite its intensity, pain is only temporary. Evil depends on our forgetting this fact. If it couldn't inflict pain, evil would have no power at all . . . . Realize that there is a reality beyond our present misery. You are that reality, and you will return to it as your suffering lessens. (p. 29)

Just as Thich Nhat Hahn happily appropriates Paul Tillich's expression "ground of being" for God, Chopra is willing to claim that that reality with which we ourselves are one, and to which Jesus

guides us – the Gnostic Christians made this especially clear – is
nothing less than "Being itself," which is another of Tillich's
formulation for the divine (p. 89). At the same time, lest we suppose
that Chopra and Nhat Hahn are in perfect agreement, we should
note that Chopra is not nearly as interested in the political
implications of spirituality as Nhat Hahn is. Chopra's contention
that Jesus taught that not just the ego, but the whole of physical
reality, is in some sense illusory contradicts Nhat Hahn's conviction
that even though the Kingdom of God announced by Jesus is within
us, life in that Kingdom ought to spur us to ethical and political
activism in the messy outer world, such as Nhat Hahn's own
activism in matters of war and peace.[22]

Indeed, Chopra sounds as if perhaps he must simply be
classified as a New Ager when he goes so far as to say that "the world
'out there' responds immediately to the world 'in here' – in other
words, outward reality mirrors the self" (p. 209). Or, again, "God-
consciousness creates its own reality" (p. 25). But, to be fair to
Chopra's approach, it should be noted that it does allow him to offer
a consistent interpretation of Jesus' extraordinarily puzzling
declaration in Matthew 6 that we ought not to worry about where
our food or clothing or shelter will come from, since God will
simply provide these things for us if we seek the Kingdom of God
(pp. 63-64).

Our brief consideration of Thich Nhat Hahn's *Living Buddha,
Living Christ* and Deepak Chopra's *The Third Jesus* finds both of
them interpreting Jesus Christ in such a way that genuine faith in
Jesus is not threatened by believers from other traditions, at least not
from the Asian traditions upon which these two authors principally
draw. What is more, there are important commonalities in how they
avoid the problem of other faiths being disconfirming to the
Christian's own belief system. For one thing, both authors
emphasize the Ultimate or God as something encountered primarily
within the depths of the self rather than as a radically transcendent
being, and the inner experiences described by the world's religions
have much more in common with one another than their
conceptual descriptions of ultimate reality. Furthermore, given their

focus upon experience and the concomitant de-emphasis upon conceptualization that goes with this inward-looking piety, these authors steer us away from the arena in which disconfirmation can even be at issue: disconfirmation is a function of propositions, and thus not of the sorts of experience that are allegedly largely ineffable. That is, the content of Hinduism, for example, that appears to contradict what Christians believe lies in what Hindus *say* about the ultimate; it lies in propositions. It does not lie in inner experiences. The very notion of disconfirmation has to do with a proposition or set of propositions contradicting other propositions. If I claim that 2 + 2 equals 3, while you say that 2 + 2 equals 4, we are contradicting one another. And to the extent that you can show me the flaw in my computation, you have disconfirmed my claim. But if I am feeling sad while you are feeling happy, we are experiencing different emotions, but it would be odd to say that we are contradicting one another, and even odder to say that you are disconfirming my emotional state.

*   *   *   *   *

But what of a popular take on our topic from the Christian side? For a Christian work aimed at a popular audience that has the potential to blunt the disconfirming effect of the Other, we look to Episcopal bishop John Shelby Spong's *Jesus for the Non-Religious*. Spong is a controversial figure within his own denomination. He has never hidden his vigorous, some might even say vitriolic, conviction that many of the theological trappings of traditional Christianity are no longer viable. Indeed, one of the constituent elements of historical Christianity that Spong is convinced collides with the sensibilities of our age is what he calls the theistic notion of God, which God he defines as a supernatural being "dwelling outside this world and able to invade the world in miraculous ways to bless, to punish, to accomplish the divine will, to answer prayers and to come to the aid of frail, powerless human beings."[23] There are echoes here of Dietrich Bonhoeffer's call for a religionless Christianity, as well as of Nietzschean and Freudian claims that traditional Christian piety is a function of weakness and immaturity, the desire for a cosmic father figure to deliver us from the slings and arrows of our finite fortune.

Yet, despite his enthusiastic denunciations of the tradition, Spong is equally enthusiastic in his claim that God is genuinely and powerfully met in the person of Jesus. As a result, his position is a strong candidate for the sort of modification strategy we are seeking, namely, one that presents the classic Christian claim that God was in Christ in a way that is not vulnerable to disconfirmation by the beliefs that constitute other world religions. This despite the fact that he himself does not wrestle with the implications of the clash of religions. Nhat Hahn explicitly juxtaposed Christ with the Buddha. Chopra sought what he took to be the real, but largely unknown Jesus, and this Jesus turned out to have much in common with Hindu and Buddhist traditions, traditions to which Chopra made explicit reference. Spong, though he does not confront his faith in Jesus Christ with the claims of other religions, tends, like Nhat Hahn and Chopra, to radically immanentize the reality of God, to make our contact with God much more a function of experience than of conceptualization, and it is of course the clash of concepts that is primarily at issue in disconfirmation. Furthermore, Spong focuses upon a Jesus who empowers this God-experience rather than upon a Jesus who becomes a sacrifice to God the Father on behalf of human sin. Given that Christian tradition ordinarily pictures the sacrifice of Jesus on the cross for our sin as an absolutely unique event that he alone can perform, deemphasizing that part of Jesus' significance also lessens the tension between devotion to Christ and the claims of other religions. And while Spong does not make the relationship between Christianity and other religions his focus, it does come up in his book, and his position on the matter is clear:

> For even Jesus, I submit, is not an end in himself, as Christians have so mistakenly assumed. Jesus is but a doorway into the wonder of God. The first followers of Jesus were not called Christians, as if knowing Christ was their goal; rather, they called themselves "the followers of

the way," as if Jesus was himself but part of their journey. The Christ path was a path toward wholeness, a journey into that which is ultimately real and for which no words have yet been devised. *All religion must ultimately flow into this same mystical reality.* (p. 137, emphasis mine)

There is a sense in which this quotation from *Jesus for the Non-Religious* summarizes Spong's entire case, a case that can be broken down into three main contentions: (1) Encountering Jesus provides the opportunity to experience God. (2) This experience of God means, concretely, that the one who has the God-experience moves toward wholeness as a human being. And (3), we have no words that can adequately or literally express this experience, and that is why mythic tales about healing, bodily resurrecting the dead, and walking on water began to be told about Jesus.

Let us consider each of these contentions in turn. First, what does Spong mean when he claims that encountering Jesus can be tantamount to encountering God? The infinite reality of God transcends all boundaries, and such transcendence of boundaries comes out concretely in the Jesus that we meet in the Gospels. In order to see how this is so, it is essential, Spong points out, to know a fair amount about the Jewish culture of Jesus' day. Spong has the deepest appreciation for that culture; he in no way wishes to denigrate it as narrow or legalistic. But we do need to acknowledge that, just as with all other cultures, including our own, the culture in which Jesus lived had its prejudices. For example, the Jews held the neighboring Samaritans in extremely low regard. Again, Jewish religious law dictated that a man could easily be ritually polluted by contact with women, for instance if a woman was menstruating. It is against this background that Jesus' parable of the Good Samaritan and his seemingly total openness to women – even including total strangers, such as the woman at the well with whom he converses, who was a Samaritan to boot (John 4:7-27) – demonstrate that Jesus broke through such prejudices. In Jesus' concrete acts of interpersonal transcendence, we encounter the unlimited power of God. Like Chopra, Spong is happy to identify this God with Paul

Tillich's "Being itself" (p. 11) (recall that Nhat Hahn embraced the parallel Tillichian formulation "ground of being").

The notion that in Jesus one encounters the power of God as Being itself provides a segue to the second contention. To see God as Being itself is to recognize God as the one who not only grants me and all other things their bare existence, but also offers me the possibility of fullness of being. While Nhat Hahn and Chopra tend to see such fullness in terms of my consciousness merging with God, Spong takes a more decidedly Western approach: he thinks in terms of psychological wholeness. The God met in Jesus offers me the opportunity to break free from the prejudices and pettiness that hold me back from the fulfilled humanity that I am meant to experience. At the same time, we ought not to draw an overly sharp distinction between what Spong has in mind in his talk of the God experience with what Nhat Hahn and Chopra intend. For as the quotation above from Spong reminds us, to experience God is to enter a "journey into that which is ultimately real and for which no words have yet been devised."

The third contention, namely, that there are no words adequate to describe the God experience is a position that Spong clearly holds in common with Thich Nhat Hahn and Deepak Chopra, but Spong adds a twist. Once again emphasizing that it is essential to understand the Jewishness of Jesus and his followers in order to decipher the Gospel accounts, Spong maintains that the early Christians and the Gospel writers reached for the literally unsayable by employing symbolic and mythic motifs fashioned from events in the Hebrew Bible and the larger Jewish tradition. For example, to say that Jesus could miraculously feed five thousand people with only a few loaves and fishes is to recall how God provided manna in the desert for the ancient Israelites, and to claim that Jesus was the "lamb of God" who miraculously removed the sins of the world is to think back both to the Paschal lamb of the Exodus and to the ritual offering of lambs in the Temple in Jerusalem. It is as if Spong wants to take us back behind Rudolf Bultmann's famous project of demythologizing the New Testament and show us how the Jesus events were mythologized in the first place. The myths and symbols are by no means simply the overenthusiastic results of the early Christians' embellishment of the Jesus stories, and they are surely not mere falsehoods. Rather, they arose because they were the most effective means at the disposal of Jesus' followers to reach beyond the inadequacies of ordinary language and its inability to communicate the *tremendum* of the Jesus encounter.

Given this summary of Spong's position, it seems that the title of his book, *Jesus for the Non-Religious*, fits his message: The Jesus that he describes, and the God met in this Jesus, can be appropriated by those who are "spiritual but not religious," which means that this Jesus is not tied to some (or perhaps any) of the specific claims of traditional, institutional Christianity that clash with central claims of the other world religions. There is no threat of disconfirmation here, since embracing Spong's Jesus does not entail holding Jesus to be the one and only atoning avenue to God, the sole door through which one can walk to spiritual fulfillment.

*   *   *   *   *

As we have proceeded in our explorations of Thich Nhat Hahn, Deepak Chopra, and John Shelby Spong, we have noted significant common features in their approaches: each thinker emphasizes the immanence of God more than God's transcendence; each holds that this immanence means that spirituality is a highly experiential undertaking; and each avers that the experience at issue cannot adequately be expressed in words.[24] It is important to note that these three interpreters were picked not because of these overlapping emphases, but simply because of their salience on the popular spiritual scene. Hence, we ought eventually to inquire about what is behind these common features, something we shall do in the following chapter.

Definitions, Essences, and Other Conundrums

By way of conclusion to the present chapter, however, there is another topic that deserves our consideration. We noted in previous chapters that, beginning several decades ago, academic commentators upon religion began to question the possibility of objectively defining religion, or whether any discrete phenomenon even exists that can be summed up under the word "religion." Jonathan Z. Smith's contention that religion is not a natural category has become the emblematic expression of this hesitation about the attempt to define religion.[25] The objection here is ordinarily not to the practical undertaking of stipulating a definition of religion to be used in a specific discussion, a contingent definition that simply highlights what is of greatest interest to a particular investigator, but in holding that it is possible to uncover some genuinely objective and irreducible essence corresponding to the word "religion" or "spirituality." The objectors claim that the ways of being to which we attach labels such as Judaism and Buddhism do not have some special set of features in common that we can self-evidently choose as the key to defining a phenomenon called "religion," a phenomenon that scholars in the past, such as Rudolf Otto and Mircea Eliade, took to be thoroughly *sui generis*, impossible to understand except on its own, essentialist terms.[26] But according to today's objectors, to talk of the essence of "religion" would be to run roughshod over the particular practices of diverse traditions.

There is both a political and a more purely academic dimension to this concern. The political concern is that, ever since the undertaking was begun in the early modern period, the thinkers who have attempted to define a general phenomenon called religion have tended to be white male Europeans or their intellectual offspring. As a result, when the general category "religion" is used as a grid to lay over individual traditions, there will be an unavoidable evaluative component in the investigation, so that when elements of Buddhism, for example, don't fit neatly into what is inevitably a biased investigation, those elements will be undervalued, if not condemned. Such use of a general, overarching definition of religion is, in the postmodern jargon, "totalizing." The academic concern, while generating less controversy, is closely related: if we begin with a definition of a general phenomenon and then use it as a grid to lay over individual traditions as a key to their meaning, we shall inevitably miss out on some of the distinctive features of those traditions.

As was mentioned in an earlier chapter, the world has been confronted in recent years with what some have called the "return of religion." And this means not just that advocates of secularization hypotheses have what appear to be counter-examples on their hands in the upsurge of traditionalist Islam and evangelical Christianity around the world. Rather, it is also the case that theorists who have been opposed to employing general, potentially totalizing definitions of religion may find their well-wrought objections simply swept away in a simultaneous resurgence of traditions from various parts of the world that suggests to the casual observer, at least, that these traditions are somehow part of a single phenomenon, that they are all instances of something that we can in fact put under the common heading "religion."

What is of interest for our purposes here is how the modification strategies that we have explored in this chapter seem to have something to offer to both sides of the argument over whether there is anything out there answering to the general category "religion." On the one hand, the whole impetus behind the modification strategies, namely, the awareness of the problem of the disconfirming Other, comes down on the side of those who want to respect the individual differences among traditions. To be troubled by the fact that my neighbor holds convictions different from my own and that I have no firmer evidence for my convictions than she has for hers is to be sensitive to the uniqueness of each tradition. If one began with the conviction that all those traditions that we call the world religions are just variations on an essentially common theme, there would be no problem of the disconfirming Other in the first place. On the other hand, the goal of the modification strategies is precisely to discover commonality, indeed a sufficiently significant commonality among religions or spiritual traditions so that one can conclude that what lies outside the circle of that commonality is not, finally, of overriding importance.

The debate about whether it is possible to define the term "religion" or "spirituality" so as to uncover an irreducible, common essence is replayed one level down, as it were, when we ask whether it is possible to define a particular religion such as "Christianity" or

"Buddhism" in such a way as to get at some "essence," at some set of characteristics without which the phenomenon in question would simply not be Christianity or Buddhism. This particular debate is relevant to our exploration of modification strategies in that there will certainly be those who will hold that the harmonizing of Christian faith with other traditions undertaken by Hick, Nhat Hahn, Chopra, and Spong has been accomplished at the unacceptable price of throwing the essence of Christianity overboard. If this charge is valid, then the approach to the disconfirming Other that we have labeled modification strategies, far from avoiding the feared disconfirmation, unintentionally abets it. Spiritual pluralism is destructive of belief in one more way, then, in that the boldest attempts to escape its disconfirming power actually destroy the individual faith that they are meant to protect.

One possible response to this complaint, a response alluded to above, is to say that we do not have to worry about the thinkers we have surveyed recasting Christian faith in a manner that destroys the essence of Christianity for the simple reason that there is no such essence. We lump together many different movements and designate them all instances of Christianity, so the argument might go, not because of some common theological core at the center of each of them, but simply because they all look to Jesus Christ as their gateway to spiritual fulfillment. Just how they understand Christ's role as this gateway varies tremendously from church to church.

Or perhaps the reason that the many different church traditions that we call Christian share that designation is, again, not because of some profound common essence, but because of Wittgensteinian family resemblances. I might say of the Smith children, "You can always spot a Smith; all of those kids are unmistakably related." But this doesn't mean that the four Smith children each have the same physical characteristics. The first Smith child and the second might share a distinctive nose and unusually dark eyes; the second child and the third might share the distinctive nose and a unique grin; the third and the fourth might have the unique grin and curly black hair. Note that in this scenario, the first Smith child and the fourth have *no* characteristics in common, yet both are still unmistakably Smiths because of the way in which specific characteristics overlap among the four children. Perhaps versions of "Christianity" are all "Christian" for the same reason. In this scenario too, there is no need to posit some common essence, and thus there is no sacrosanct set of essential principles that the authors we have explored have abandoned. Certainly the versions of devotion to Jesus set forth by Thich Nhat Hahn, Deepak Chopra, and John Shelby Spong have at least some characteristics that overlap with other forms of devotion that have, over the long haul of history, been designated "Christian."

What may be more significant than such defenses against the destruction-of-essence charge, however, is to recognize that the challenge posed by spiritual pluralism changes the significance of the very notion of the essence of Christianity, or of any other faith. Most persons with an investment in the idea that Christianity has a discernable essence, something that endures over time despite external changes, have a potent interest in the truth question. That is, they are Christians who believe that the Christian faith is a function of divine revelation and a secure pathway to salvation. The concern is that if one deviates from the essence of Christian belief, one falsifies the Christian tradition and loses contact with the divine truth that genuine Christianity has to offer. If the modification strategies outlined above have abandoned the essence of Christianity, they have also forfeited its truth.

But we need to recall the nature of the pluralistic challenge. I might begin with confidence that the Christian faith I embrace is unquestionably an expression of some discernable essence of Christianity. But when I recognize that those of other faiths have convictions that contradict my own and that the grounds for those convictions are every bit as solid as what grounds my belief, I face disconfirmation. Whether or not my version of Christian faith captures what I have hitherto confidently embraced as the eternal essence of Christianity, I confront the mathematical odds to which we have so frequently referred before: the odds are that my faith convictions are false.

If follows from this that the loss-of-essence problem must take second place to the challenge of the disconfirming Other. But suppose that I identify a modification strategy that I am convinced meets the Other's challenge. If I have taken that all-important step, surely *then* it is reasonable to examine the Christian faith with which that modification strategy leaves me and ask whether it is sufficiently close to the faith with which I began that this modified faith is worth holding onto. Without reentering the fray about whether notions such as the essence of Christianity make sense, there is one particular question that many a Christian who contemplates the modification strategies represented by Nhat Hahn, Chopra, and Spong will surely ask themselves: Is it acceptable to abandon the theme of Jesus Christ's atoning death on the cross as God's once-and-for-all conquest of human sin?

Granted, atonement for sin is not the only task that traditional Christianity equates with the role of Jesus Christ. The contemporary *Catechism of the Catholic Church* lists the following reasons for the incarnation of God in Jesus Christ: *"in order to save us by reconciling us with God," "so that we might know God's love," "to be our model of holiness,"* and to make us *"'partakers of the divine nature'"* (the last phrase is quoted from 2nd Peter 1:4).[27] There is no surprise, however, that atonement or "reconciliation" leads this list. The other tasks associated with the Christ's incarnation appear, at least at first blush, to be shareable with other redeemer figures, especially if one recalls Nhat Hahn's willingness to interpret Buddhism, which is usually taken as non-theistic, as offering something akin to the indwelling of the Holy Spirit in the spiritual quester. But can one who wants to maintain his or her identity as a Christian adopt a modification strategy that foregoes the cross as atonement? It would seem unlikely, and if it in fact cannot be done then pluralism will indeed prove a challenge to belief: without a modification strategy, pluralism pits religions against one another so that they essentially cancel each other out. But with a modification strategy that overcomes pluralism's threat of disconfirmation, one's faith may end up being unrecognizable and perhaps no longer worth affirming.

At the same time, however, changes in American culture over the years have rendered the notion that we are caught up in sin much less salient, even for pious Christians. Thus it is that the psychologist Karl Menninger could ask, as early as 1973, in the title of a book, *Whatever Became of Sin?*[28] Could it be, then, that tasks other than atonement assigned to Jesus Christ by the Christian tradition, tasks that appear to be kept intact in the modification strategies of Nhat Hahn, Chopra, and Spong, will be sufficient for many Christians? One would be unwise to bet on such a scenario. Indeed, it is advisable to recall one of the Christian tradition's most venerable insights about how it crafts its theological doctrines, namely, that the *lex credendi* follows the *lex orandi*: the law of believing, of doctrinal affirmation, follows the law of praying. That is, the Christian church's central theological doctrines were not spun out by theologians (nor revealed to them) with the Christian liturgy faithfully following and expressing those doctrines. Rather, it more often works the other way around: the concrete, day-to-day worship practices of the faithful stimulate theological reflection and explanation. Christians were baptizing infants before theologians worked out the details of infant baptism as a sacrament that washes away the effects of original sin.

Now consider the fact that the central worship practice of Christianity's largest body, the Roman Catholic Church, is the sacrifice of the Mass. The Catholic liturgy is built around Jesus' sacrificial, atoning death on the cross. Thus, even if contemporary Christians are less likely than their foremothers and forefathers to dwell on the idea that the human condition is constantly threatened by sin and guilt, it is hard to imagine casting aside Jesus' role as the sacrificial lamb of God who takes away the sins of the world. Every time a Christian, Roman Catholic or otherwise, participates in Holy Communion, which most Protestant Christians too consider a sacrament initiated by Jesus himself, Jesus' identification with atonement is reinforced.

On the one hand, it would be foolish to suppose that there is absolutely no way in which the traditional emphasis upon Christ's sacrificial role can be integrated with the picture of Christ that follows from embracing the modification strategies. For instance, one might begin by noting that in all of the world religions, the world is regarded as somehow "out of joint," as the Buddhists put it; there is something fundamentally wrong with the way in which human beings relate to reality. Nhat Hahn, Chopra, and Spong all lay out their proposals in a way that allows us to look at reality at least quasi-theistically. Hahn's comments on the Kingdom of God and the Holy Spirit make it clear that even a Buddhist can make sense of theistic language, though perhaps it would be most accurate to say that God-language can be taken by a Buddhist such as Nhat Hahn as symbolic speech that can be translated into language more familiar to Buddhists. In any case, given this general commitment to the meaningfulness of God-language, it is possible to view the world's being out of joint as tied up with human estrangement from God. The various spiritual quests that the world religions preach would not need to be so difficult, so rigorous, and so constant if we were not separated from the divine ground of our being. Therefore, religion and spirituality must offer some way in which to overcome this separation.

A goodly number of rabbis will tell us that such reconciliation is in our own hands: no matter how sinful we are, we can take comfort in the teaching about *teshuvah* or "turning" back to God: we always have it in our power to turn back to God, no matter how badly we have lived our lives. Most other world religions will probably agree with this sentiment, or at least with some variation upon it. Again, symbolic translation may be required when a religion such as Buddhism or Taoism encounters this sort of God-language. In Taoism, for instance, the "estrangement" is that of the human self or ego from the Way of the universe. One can overcome this estrangement by emptying oneself of one's egotistical projects and harmonizing oneself with the Tao so that one's actions are a function of the Tao flowing through the self.

As it turns out, the traditional Christian must also engage in some symbolic translation if he or she wishes to embrace both the modification strategies and the notion of Christ's death as an atoning sacrifice. That is, he or she must be able to take the traditional language of atonement and see it as having dimensions beyond its most unimaginative, literal meaning. But perhaps this is not quite as difficult a maneuver as it first appears. For the problem actually lies with one particular interpretation of that atoning sacrifice that has been worked out in Western Christianity. By far the dominant interpretation of the cross is based on the famous argument set forth by Anselm of Canterbury in his *Cur Deus Homo?*[29] That argument suggests that the atonement was an objective process, something akin to a legal proceeding that took place between God the Father and God the Son, rather than an event that effected a subjective process, a change within the human heart. Human beings are debtors before the Father in as much as the Father has been done a grave injustice by human sin. Christ the Son gives himself to the Father as a sacrifice that pays that debt. In the Anselmian picture, Christ's sacrifice is a thoroughly unique, one-time intervention on behalf of all humanity that provides for the possibility of human salvation from sin. Hence, given the Anselmian model, it appears to be impossible to square Christ's role as savior from sin with the perspective derived from the modification strategies emerging from the books by Hahn, Chopra, and Spong.

But the Anselmian interpretation of the cross is not the only interpretation available. For instance, in the twelfth century, the century following Anselm's own, the theologian Peter Abelard proposed what is often called the "moral influence" theory of atonement. Here, the atoning power of the cross is not to be found in a supernatural transaction between God the Father and God the Son but rather in a straightforward interaction between Christ and individual human beings. Christ is the preeminent revelation of God, and he brings the message of God's love for humanity. Because Jesus Christ is himself God in the flesh, the cross makes apparent the extraordinary lengths to which God will go in the name of this love for us. The individual seeker, contemplating this demonstration of unconditional divine love, will be moved to accept God's offer of grace which will allow him or her to live in obedience to God and in fellowship with other human beings.

If our hypothetical twenty-first-century Christian adopts Abelard's view of the cross, then he or she can also embrace the modification strategies. First of all, the picture of the cross as an instrument that reaches deep into the human heart and turns estranged humans back to God can easily be integrated into the modification strategies' notion of the ultimate and the centrality of our consciousness of it. Second, because Jesus' death on the cross now need not be regarded as an essential, one-time transaction between the Father and the Son on behalf of all of humanity, the claim of its absolute uniqueness can also be abandoned. Hence, the cross might be regarded by Christians as one powerful way in which God penetrates the human heart, a way that is not in competition with other ways in which the ultimate breaks down our hardheartedness, such as the teachings of the Buddha or the yogic paths offered by Indian religion. In this way, it is only the claim that the cross is a unique necessity that is left behind. The cross is an extraordinarily powerful way – one way among several others – via which our inadequate God-consciousness, the source of our sin, can be repaired.

In any case, the proposals set forth by Nhat Hahn, Chopra, and Spong are sufficiently suggestive with regard to our primary topic, the threat of the disconfirming Other, that we need to analyze the three motifs that their work shares – the immanence of the ultimate, the importance of experience in knowing that ultimate, and the ineffability of the ultimate – in greater detail and to push deeper into what their proposals portend for pluralism. That will be the task of the next chapter.

CHAPTER FOUR

Modification Strategies:
Their Elements and Their Social Context

At the outset of our study, we explored several tactics that are essentially attempts to avoid the challenge of the disconfirming Other, namely, compartmentalization, the eschewal of logic where spiritual matters are concerned, and self-deception, along with the oppositional strategy that is fundamentalism. Then, in Chapter Three, we concentrated on modification strategies that attempt to meet the pluralistic challenge head-on. To the extent that these modification strategies initially appear to be successful in dealing with the challenge of the disconfirming Other, it behooves us to push further in our investigation of them. That further investigation should give us insight not only into the specifics of how the modification strategies are constructed, but also into how their constituent elements are part of the larger American culture.

Furthermore, given the fact that the phenomenon of religious pluralism is our focus, we must investigate other relationships that the modification strategies have to American spiritual and religious pluralism beyond warding off disconfirmation. On this last matter, I shall argue that modification strategies find themselves in a circular relationship with American spiritual pluralism, a relationship of reciprocal causation. First of all, the very characteristics that power the modification strategies and thus protect belief from the disconfirmation threatened by pluralism draw upon that pluralism as conditions of their own possibility. And, secondly, the modification strategies themselves add to the very pluralism that makes them necessary.

The popular modification strategies that we considered shared a number of significant characteristics. Thich Nhat Hahn, Deepak Chopra, and John Shelby Spong all embraced approaches to spirituality, and to Jesus Christ in particular, that emphasized divine *immanence* over transcendence, that focused on *experience* rather than on the explicitly reflective or the deed-oriented elements of spirituality, and that claimed that the experience of the ultimate is often *ineffable*, that is, that it cannot adequately be expressed in words. These three characteristics are, of course, tightly linked to one another: It makes sense to suppose that I might be able to experience the ultimate if it is truly immanent, whereas I might not be able to experience a radically transcendent ultimate. Furthermore, while the cognitive dimension of spirituality can, perhaps by definition, be put into words (concepts being dependent upon language), what we are here calling "experience" can be construed, especially if it is a particular sort of experience, as something that words cannot adequately express. The two professional religious thinkers whom we briefly considered in our investigation of modification strategies, namely, Karl Rahner and John Hick, present a less unified perspective on immanence, experience, and ineffability in their work, and we shall have something to say about their approaches later on.

Let us begin, however, with a more detailed investigation of what we have identified as the three defining emphases of the popular strategies that we have considered. Our first topic is immanence. It seems likely that spirituality and religion have almost perennially displayed a dialectic of immanence and transcendence. There are numerous examples to be found in the world's spiritualities of a dynamic in which a high god, a creator god who is often believed to reside in the sky, is understood as radically transcendent, and more attention is paid to other, more immanent manifestations of the divine as a result of the human desire to be in contact with ultimate reality. For instance, we find anthropological accounts of African traditions that believe in a God that is sufficiently transcendent that this deity becomes of little day-to-day significance among its people, so that worship and invocation are directed to intermediary forces or beings instead.[1] Along the same lines, the influential sociologist Max Weber famously speaks of the "disenchantment" of the world that he sees effected by both Judaism and Protestantism.[2] Judaism arises in a world where there are, among Israel's neighbors and perhaps initially among the Israelites themselves, a host of immanent deities, manifestations of the ultimate that are found in sacred objects such as statues – recall the Israelites' own infamous lapse into idolatry in the Golden Calf story in the Hebrew Bible (Exodus 32) – and in the world of nature, as evidenced by the notion of sacred powers that fructify the earth. But Hebrew theology, at least at some point in its development, attempts mightily to oppose these radically immanent deities in favor of a more transcendent (and singular) God. Where the notion takes hold that divine reality is to be found only in the ineffable Yahweh, a God sufficiently transcendent that no human being can see him face-to-face and live and whose name, "I Am," is essentially the mysterious refusal of a name, then the world here below is effectively bereft of supernatural realities. This is what Weber had in mind when speaking of disenchantment.

Christianity begins as a Jewish sect, but its central claim, namely, that God has become incarnate in the man Jesus offers the possibility of re-enchanting the world. Yet Jesus too can become a remote figure, as when he is depicted as the fierce *Pantocrator* (Ruler of All) who shall preside over the Final Judgment, in which a vast number of souls will be condemned to eternal damnation. It has often been observed that the remoteness of God, even in his form as the Christ if Christ be conceived as the *Pantocrator,* gave rise to the whole apparatus of sacraments and devotion to Mary and the saints that arose within Roman Catholicism, for these all suggest a more available divine. The dialectic of transcendence and immanence has here effected a move from the original Jewish emphasis upon transcendence to a much greater emphasis upon immanence: to the extent that God the Father and the ascended Son become remote and intimidating, ordinary piety turns to more immediate representatives of the supernatural.

But some forms of Protestantism continue the dialectic by disenchanting the world once more. Particularly in its Calvinist form, Protestantism eschews veneration of the saints and Mary as tantamount to idolatry.[3] While it hardly negates all immanence, given its continuing emphasis upon the Incarnation of God in Christ, its actual worship practices and iconography – or perhaps more accurately, its striking lack of iconography – swing back in the direction of the transcendent.

The fact that the back-and-forth between transcendence and immanence is indeed, at least in some instances, a "dialectic" is highlighted in Mark C. Taylor's reading of twentieth-century Christian thought:

> The history of theology in the West . . . is the story of repeated "altarnation" [from the Latin for "other"] between monisms in which the real is immanent, that is, in some way *present* here and now, and dualisms in which the real is transcendent, that is, *absent* or, more precisely, present elsewhere. Appearances to the contrary notwithstanding, these theological alternatives are not simply opposites but are dialectically related in such a way that, when either is pushed to its limit, it negates itself and turns into the other. In the course of the twentieth century, the immanence of liberalism gives way to the transcendence of neoorthodoxy, which, in turn, is negated by the death of God theology. For many religious conservatives, the death of God was symptomatic of the relativism and nihilism of the sixties. The recent emergence of neofoundationalism represents the effort to reverse this perceived decline by reasserting religious and moral absolutes.[4]

If there appears to be an ongoing dialectic of transcendence and immanence, then, in the history of religions and spiritualities, it makes sense to ask whether there are factors in contemporary cultures, especially the United States, that presently favor the note of immanence. For if there are, this would help explain the character of the modification strategies that we have examined by establishing that the emphasis upon immanence is ready-to-hand in contemporary American culture.

Surely there are such immanence-privileging factors. We begin with the philosophical environment in which modern Christian theology came to birth. The bulk of modern philosophy, as initiated by René Descartes, is indelibly marked by the famous "turn to the subject." According to this sensibility, philosophizing (and perhaps also theologizing) ought to start with the knowing subject rather than with what is alleged to be known. Immanuel Kant argued, persuasively for many, that we can know things only as they have always already been worked over by our mental apparatus, never as they are in and of themselves. If religious thinkers take this turn to the subject seriously, as many of them have done from the nineteenth century to the present, then our ability to know God or the ultimate will always be a knowing "from below." God cannot in this case be absolutely other, for there must be something in the very constitution of the human subject that provides a point of contact for encountering the divine and that dictates that the divine does indeed have an immanent dimension. It is worth noting that Friedrich Schleiermacher and Johann Adam Möhler, a Protestant and a Roman Catholic respectively, turned out to be two of the most influential religious thinkers of the nineteenth century, and that both set forth theologies based upon an examination of the human subject's inherent capacity to intuit the divine.

While Karl Barth and his followers attempted to steer theology away from the turn to the subject, American religious thought has tended, throughout the modern period and into our own time, to be guided by that historic turn and, thus, to privilege the immanent dimension of the divine over the transcendent. Hence, some of the most influential works of twentieth-century theology in America were produced by thinkers such as David Tracy and Sallie McFague, both of whom self-consciously address epistemological issues and have clearly imbibed something of the subjective turn, especially in their earlier work.[5] It should be noted, in addition, that even postmodern thinkers who abandon the turn to the subject (thanks in large part to Martin Heidegger's critique of the human subject's attempts at cognitive mastery and the consequent forgetfullness of Being) can continue to emphasize an immanent divinity. Witness Mark C. Taylor's equation of language with the divine milieu in which all things arise and pass away.[6]

Of greater importance than the philosophers' turn to the subject, however, is the emphasis upon democracy, egalitarianism, and individuality in American culture. There is perhaps no more paradigmatically American novel than Ralph Ellison's *Invisible Man* (1952), in which the protagonist is advised to be his own father, to create himself. Ellison's radically existentialist take on the human condition may well rule out a decidedly spiritual or religious perspective. But Americans who do embrace a spiritual vision will likely bring to that vision an Ellisonian emphasis upon the necessity of being true to one's own values and perspective. And, of course, it is worth noting that Ellison's full name was in fact Ralph *Waldo* Ellison, and that his namesake Ralph Waldo Emerson's championing of self-reliance ended up including the conviction that God was very immanent indeed, that the individual human being was an organ of the divine. The Transcendentalist movement, of which Emerson is the most distinguished representative, focused upon the immediacy of the divine to the human. The emphases upon egalitarianism and self-reliance that permeate American culture and that are enshrined in the thought of Emerson mean that even theologies that are not concerned with academic debates about the turn to the subject will very likely emphasize divine immanence of one sort or another. Rosemary Radford Ruether's notion of the divine as the "Primal Matrix" that embraces men and women in the down-to-earth circumstances and struggles of their everyday lives, along with the world of nature, qualifies as a significant example.[7]

That a sense of divine immanence, indeed a conviction that human beings actually participate in divinity, has been at the heart of American piety for some time is the burden of Harold Bloom's *The American Religion*.[8] Bloom is at his best here, for, like one of his heroes, Sigmund Freud, he reaches for the big hypothesis, the grandiose claim, and spares his readers the qualifications and caveats that punctuate the flow of the argument in much scholarly work. According to Bloom, distinctly American religions such as Mormonism, the Southern Baptist churches, and Christian Science are animated by the conviction that the human soul is older than creation: we are closer to divinity than to the finite, created order. And Bloom claims that this conviction has not been confined to religions born on these shores, but has had an impact on many traditional European religions as they have become acculturated to the American scene, even religions such as Roman Catholicism and Lutheranism. The conviction that the soul is older than creation is in the spiritual atmosphere that Americans of all stripes breathe.

We return to our earlier observation, then, that the notion of divine immanence is ready-to-hand to those who, in today's America, wish to embrace a modification strategy designed to avoid disconfirmation by the Other. And, of course, not only is the idea of divine immanence readily available to the contemporary American spiritual quester, it has peculiar strengths in dealing with religious and spiritual pluralism, as we have seen, and thus will be particularly attractive to those questers whose focal concern is to avoid disconfirmation by the Other.

An emphasis upon experience is the second hallmark of the modification strategies that we have examined. Thich Nhat Hahn goes so far as to assert that "Authentic experience makes a religion a true religion."[9] The focus upon experience fits seamlessly with the emphasis on divine immanence: if the divine is not distant from us but, rather, close by, then we can do more than simply represent it to ourselves via concepts or behave according to moral dictates that we believe to be divine demands: we can encounter the divine more directly, specifically through our own "experience."

The word "experience" is used in so many different ways and in so many diverse contexts, however, that we need to examine it in more detail and specify its meaning as used in the modification strategies with which we are concerned here. Suppose that I am asked by a friend, "Have you ever experienced white-water rafting?" I will say "No," even though I know what that kind of rafting is and have frequently seen television and movie footage of people engaged in it. For me to be able to say that I have actually "experienced" white-water rafting requires that I have engaged in that activity myself. In other words, "experience" suggests actual participation, and the sort of participation that is involved in the case of rafting is physical and vigorous.

By contrast, consider the case where I inquire of a friend, "Have you ever had the experience of seeing the *Mona Lisa*?" She will probably only answer my question affirmatively if she has been to the Louvre and looked at the actual painting. In this instance, however, experience is not tied up with vigorous activity, but it does once again suggest proximity, an intimate participation in something: she must have seen the original painting with her own eyes, not just reproductions of it, in order to claim to have had the experience.

If experience demands proximity to or some sort of participation in a particular phenomenon, it is even more obvious that it demands an accompanying consciousness. If I were loaded onto a white-water raft while in a coma and remained comatose throughout the raft's journey, I would not be able to claim upon coming out of my coma that I had experienced rafting, even though one might argue that, at least in a weak sense, I had participated in it; certainly I was proximate to the phenomenon. Thus, experience in the relevant sense demands not just proximity and not just any sort of participation, but participation in the sense of being consciously involved in a phenomenon.

Our analysis of experience thus far is consistent with Kant's definition of it as "knowledge by means of connected perceptions."[10] Both the words "knowledge" and "perception" in his formula are functions of consciousness. Perception as Kant understands it is given through sensible intuition. Whether I am white-water rafting or gazing at a famous painting, my experience will be dependent upon the five senses. But the notion of "actually experiencing" something as opposed to merely being acquainted with it from a distance often includes not just the input that is sensible intuition and the proximity to an object that sensible intuition presupposes but also certain accompanying subjective states, most obviously what we call "emotions" or "feelings." Thus, to "really experience" white-water rafting in the sense in which we are ordinarily inclined to employ that phrase includes the fact that braving the river produces in one a sense of excitement and adventure, or perhaps of terror. As for one's seeing the actual *Mona Lisa*, that experience could be accompanied by a state of boredom and thus lead to the conclusion that the painting is highly overrated. But such disappointment and boredom are nonetheless part of what defines the experience.

Our authors' emphasis on "experience" in their modification strategies suggests proximity to and participation in ultimate reality, then, along with a subjective state that the experiencer reads as consistent with such contact with the ultimate . But in the case of spiritual or religious experience, the subjective states may well take on a different and much more important role than they have in our examples of experiencing rafting and a famous painting. A cursory consideration of the experience of white-water rafting and of seeing the *Mona* Lisa suggests that the subjective states are *caused by* one's rafting or seeing the *Mona Lisa*, though the states exist in the midst of the rafting or the viewing of a painting. In other words, I still need to have the subjective states in order to have the full-blown experiences of rafting and viewing the *Mona Lisa,* but there will be a definite causal order such that the subjective states are results of my braving the river's currents or of my placing myself in front of the painting. But where ultimate reality is concerned, the reality that Thich Nhat Hahn, Deepak Chopra, and John Shelby Spong are all happy to call the Ground of Being or Being-itself, the object of the experience is not a physical phenomenon. I cannot touch it or see it and, as a result, be put into a particular subjective state. It seems, rather, that the subjective state or states will have to be intuitive in the relevant technical philosophical sense: those states themselves will need to be interpreted as the reception of something given to the mind, in this case the reality of Being-itself. A subjective sense of overwhelming mystery, for example, might be the way in which I claim that God or Being-itself shows itself to me, rather than simply my response to being in the divine presence.

What we have here is an instance of what can be called "intuitive internal experience," insofar as the subjective or internal states are intuitive and thus definitive of the experience.[11] As internal, they obviously pass the test of proximity or participation. Of course, the skeptic can immediately contest the claim that such internal experiences are intuitive rather than simply generated by one's own mind. Or, if the skeptic is inclined to grant that such internal experiences can be intuitive, that they can present something to the mind that stands outside it, he or she will undoubtedly point out that we cannot be certain just what reality they are presenting. I don't have to conclude, for instance, that the experience of radical mystery puts me in touch with Being-itself.

But however one decides to evaluate the trustworthiness of what we have decided to call intuitive internal experience, it is nonetheless evident, I think, that the emphasis upon piety as intuitive internal experience is, like the note of divine immanence, ready-to-hand in contemporary American culture. George Lindbeck's *The Nature of Doctrine* underlines this point. In Chapter Three, we examined Lindbeck's notion of a spirituality or religion as a cultural-linguistic construction, a discrete world with internal principles that dictate the meaning of assertions and behaviors. We found Lindbeck's cultural-linguistic approach vulnerable to the disconfirming Other and, thus, not a viable interpretation of spirituality and religion for one who wishes to craft a modification strategy addressing pluralism's challenge to belief. But while the cultural-linguistic perspective is the one that Lindbeck himself advocates, it is not the only perspective that he analyzes. He recognizes two major alternative approaches to spirituality among theologians, namely, the "cognitive-propositional" approach and the "experiential-expressive" one. It is the latter that seems to be presupposed in the writing of Nhat Hahn, Chopra, and Spong. Lindbeck provides a useful description of experiential-expressivism, which he grants has been the regnant model in modern and contemporary theology. More specifically, he provides a description of it that makes evident experiential-expressivism's potential appeal to anyone seeking to find unity among different religious or spiritual traditions. Most basically, the experiential-expressivist will "locate ultimately significant contact with whatever is finally important to religion in the prereflective experiential depths of the self [this surely suggests what we have called "intuitive internal experience"] and regard the public or outer features of religion as expressive and evocative objectifications (i.e., nondiscursive symbols) of internal experience."[12] What is more, "Different religions are diverse expressions or objectifications of a common core experience."[13] That is, since the core of religion or spirituality is an internal experience and religious doctrines and rubrics are simply outward expressions of this inner experience, and because such outward expressions can never do justice to the actual experience, different traditions might very well be pointing to the exact same experience despite expressing it in different words or acts.

Further evidence that, especially where the spiritual quest is concerned, an emphasis upon intuitive internal experience is endemic to contemporary American culture can be had by noting that, beginning in the 1960s, Americans have displayed an insatiable appetite for mystical religious traditions, from Hindu and Buddhist meditation-centered varieties to historic Christian mysticism as exemplified by John of the Cross and Julian of Norwich to the Jewish Kabala.[14] That American questers have often, in the interest of instant gratification, watered down these classical mysticisms, sometimes to the point of inanity, is not of concern to us here: we are simply noting yet another indication of the ready-to-hand character of an emphasis upon internal experience in the spiritual journey.

The notion of intuitive internal spiritual experience is only an intellectual stone's throw away from the claim of ineffability, which is the third distinguishing mark of the popular modification strategies that we have investigated. The writers whom we have considered appear to hold that an immanent ultimate can be given to consciousness in intuitive internal experience, but that neither the object of such experience nor even the experience itself can adequately be described via the conceptual tools available to finite human beings. Theology is frequently a waste of time. Better simply to open oneself to the experience. Of course, much depends upon the word "adequately" in the expression "adequately described," for, after all, if it were impossible to understand or to communicate about the experience of the ultimate in any fashion whatsoever, then there could be no books such as *Living Buddha, Living Christ*; *The Third Jesus*; and *Jesus for the Non-Religious*. For the ultimate to be totally ineffable, in other words, would mean that we could never encounter it, for there would be nothing for our minds to grasp. Nothing would be given to consciousness. We must be able to understand something about the reality in question even to claim that it is ultimate and (to a large extent) ineffable.

Christian theologians, in particular, have long wrestled with the challenge of how little we apparently know about God and what we can in fact say about God. They have come up with at least three possible ways to proceed. Perhaps, given God's infinity and our finitude, we can only say what God is not. Thus, the familiar Christian claim that "God is love" really means no more than that God has no characteristics contrary to love. A second possibility is that, in addition to saying what God is not, we can say what God is in relation to us. In this case, "God is love" is not talking about the inner being of the divine, something far beyond our ken, but is describing the loving, compassionate way in which believers experience God acting toward them. The third possibility thinks of our statements about God as symbolic (note that Lindbeck links this recourse to symbolism with experiential-expressivism in the quotation above).

Of course, "symbolic" is another slippery term. Even if we confine it to just one of its possible meanings, namely, analogy, we must be satisfied with choosing one possible interpretation among others, since analogy has been variously understood by different Christian thinkers down through the centuries. Here is one representative interpretation of analogical language: to say that "God is love" means that, while we can never grasp God's infinite and perfect love, we can say with confidence that it is at least something like human love. Succinctly put, to say that "God is love," then, means that God is a loving being (or the loving ground of being) akin to the fashion in which my best friend Jamie is a loving being, except that God's love is free of any limitation or imperfection. Because the human mind cannot grasp love that is free of limitation or imperfection, analogical language about God still has a good deal of modesty attached to it.

What does all of this mean for the claim made by Nhat Hahn, Chopra, and Spong that the ultimate is somehow ineffable? We have already suggested that they hold that the ultimate is given to consciousness in certain experiences, which experiences necessarily have an internal, emotional component. They go on to say that there is much about this ultimate, the Ground of Being or Being-itself, that escapes the conceptual tools available to finite human beings. This large degree of incomprehensibility means that the experiences through which the ultimate is given to consciousness are themselves only vaguely describable, more difficult to describe, that is, than ordinary subjective states. While we have all had experiences of inner peace, for example, these garden-variety experiences of peace do not begin to approach the power of the experience of unconditional peace that the spiritual seeker claims to have had. The latter is what St. Paul refers to as the "peace that surpasses all understanding" (Philippians 4:7).

Just where does the phenomenon of symbolism (in the form of analogy explained above) come into play, then? Let us say that our hypothetical spiritual seeker has an experience of unconditional peace (a large component of which is the cognitively negative and hence humble experience of being unable to find any gaps in the experience of peace; our seeker can detect no portion of his or her selfhood left untouched by this experience). Let us suppose, furthermore, that the seeker in question is a Christian (so that she identifies the source of unconditional peace with Jesus Christ as the revelation, indeed the presence, of God) and that she wants to tell me of her experience. It is unlikely that she will start right off with symbolic talk: she will not look at me and blurt out "Jesus is the Good Shepherd" (see John 10:11). Rather, she will begin speaking literally, in a manner something like the following: "I felt that I was directly in touch with Christ. An indescribable feeling of peace came over me. It was as if I was being sustained by Christ in such a way that nothing could ever harm me, or even cause me worry, ever again. The feeling was so intense, I really can't describe it." This attempted description makes use of language not about God or Christ *in themselves*, but of Christ's peace-giving *relationship* to the experiencer. It is followed by the quite literal confession that the experience was sufficiently intense and unique that the experiencer has no adequate way literally to describe it.

At another moment in her Christian practice, however, the subject of this experience may well feel herself particularly drawn to the biblical affirmation, attributed to Jesus himself, that Jesus is the Good Shepherd. Indeed, it may become for her the most powerful of Jesus' "I am" statements, given its ability to suggest Jesus' care for his followers, a care that inspires a sense of peace. Jesus' affirmation is clearly symbolic or, to revert to the terminology we have used previously, analogical. As far as we know, the historical man Jesus of Nazareth was not a shepherd. But we are talking, in any case, about an experience not of the historical Jesus but of Jesus as the eternal presence of God. Thus, the statement, "Jesus is the Good Shepherd" is a symbolic or analogical statement in the requisite sense for our purposes: it allows the experiencer to say something about the extraordinary experience of inner peace that she attributes to Jesus Christ but does so with the noetic modesty characteristic of analogy, since Jesus Christ is not literally a shepherd.

What does all of this have to do with the attraction to analogy on the part of our advocates of modification strategies? If a Christian avers that "Jesus is the Good Shepherd" as the result of her spiritual experience and a Buddhist tells us that, given his experience, the ultimate is like a body of perfectly pure water whose glassy surface is undisturbed by so much as a ripple, the two questers need not be seen as threatening to disconfirm one another's sense of the ultimate. In other words, two symbolic statements, unlike two literal ones, can draw on very different material without contradicting one another in any way. If I say in one stanza of a poem that my true love is like a star shining down from the heavens and in another stanza that she is like a dew-covered rose, I can fairly be accused of writing bad poetry, but not of contradicting myself.

*   *   *   *   *

Thus far, this chapter has provided the occasion to look at the defining emphases of the modification strategies advanced by Nhat Hahn, Chopra, and Spong in some detail and to note the ready-to-hand character of those emphases in the larger American culture. Before we move on to a consideration of some additional ways in which these same emphases are connected to pluralism, i.e., ways beyond simply warding off the disconfirmation threatened by spiritual pluralism, we need briefly to return to the two professional religious thinkers whom we also considered in the previous chapter. Karl Rahner set forth what we categorized as a spiritual inclusivism, while John Hick provided an example of a pluralist theology. To what extent is their thought too driven by the elements of immanence, experience, and ineffability?

The philosophical foundations of Rahner's theology that were of concern to us displayed all three with great clarity. What God could possibly be more immanent than Rahner's God, who makes himself present to us as an *a priori* condition for the possibility of any human mental act? This God is, in the words of the Quran, closer to us than our jugular vein (50:16).[15] And while we did not go on to discuss the sort of religious experience that Rahner attaches to so-called "special revelation," the thematic revelation he believes was provided to humanity in Jesus Christ, the ever-immanent God who communicates himself in the constitution of our consciousness is also ever an object of our experience, albeit unthematically. Every waking hour, we possess a pre-grasp of the being of God. And, finally, Rahner is emphatic in his assertion that this same God who is ever-present to all human beings is "holy mystery," an infinite far beyond our means of comprehension. That is, Rahner avers that, where Christian theology is concerned, an emphasis upon immanence need not rule out an equally ardent emphasis upon transcendence.

John Hick presents a bit more complex case. According to the scenario that he suggests, during Jasper's "Axial Period," the ultimate presented itself in several cultures around the world. On the one hand, Hick does appear to assume that this meant that the different spiritual seers behind the various world religions did indeed each have an *experience* of the divine. They did not simply philosophize about the divine or draw conclusions about human responsibilities implied by the existence of the divine. On the other hand, he does not accept the claim that, at root, all of these experiences of ultimate reality were one and the same and that the differences among the world religions resulted from subsequent choices about how to express this single experience of the ultimate. Instead, he argues that the experiences had by the original seers were themselves different, because the seers came into the presence of divinity already conditioned by the multi-faceted characteristics of their diverse cultures. Hence, for example, some prophets and seers experienced the divine from the beginning as personal, while others experienced it as an impersonal Absolute.

Of course, at the end of the day, this contrast with the one-experience-many-expressions formula at the heart of our three paradigmatic popular modification strategies may be a distinction without a difference. For Hick goes on to claim that the different cultural lenses that the religious pioneers brought to their encounter with the ultimate meant that they were not experiencing the ultimate as it is in itself – the noumenal ultimate – but only the ultimate as it appears through those lenses – the phenomenal ultimate. Therefore, despite the religions' different foundational experiences, all of those experiences were in fact of the same ultimate reality. As a result, Hick too can finally claim that the contradictory theologies of the different world religions are not really fatally contradictory after all, for – and this is a move that connects Hick's discussion with the notion of ineffability – those theologies are merely phenomenal adumbrations that, as such, may contradict one another with regard to their phenomenal claims without actually being in disagreement about the noumenal reality to which they point.

Hence, it appears that the familiar emphases on experience and an element of ineffability are both present in Hick's proposal. However, one possible interpretation of Hick's approach is that the experiential element was really only of definitive significance for the founders of the various traditions: these founders had their religious experiences and then formed systems of belief and ritual based upon those experiences. And this might mean, in turn, that for the followers down through the ages, in distinction to the founders, internal, intuitive experience of the ultimate does not really come into play. Rather, these followers' lives are formed by the belief and ritual systems handed down to them. Of course, the beliefs and rituals inspire experiences in the followers, some of which are no doubt powerful, but these experiences might well be interpreted as emotional responses to the beliefs and rites, not intuitive phenomena via which the ultimate is given to consciousness. If this be the case, then experience is not as important a player in Hick's version of things as it is in the thought of Nhat Hahn, Chopra, and Spong.

But what of the remaining characteristic, namely, immanence? Once again, it is possible to read Hick in a way that does not put the same emphasis on divine immanence that our other authors have. For, to the extent that the ordinary religious person's piety is largely determined by the belief system that has been handed down to him or her and not to his or her own intuitive experience of the divine, it is quite possible that that very belief system will emphasize divine transcendence at the expense of divine immanence. Remember our observation in the previous chapter that Hick's theology proceeds largely "from above" rather than "from below." The divine seeks out prophets who can communicate something of divine reality to the larger human community, rather than the divine being ever-present to each and every human being given the very constitution of human nature. Of course, the formative prophets themselves must be able claim that God was immanent for them, at least at those moments in which they were receiving their purported revelations.

Despite Hick's standing as something of an "odd man out," however, we must recall that his noumenal/phenomenal distinction allows one to avoid the disconfirmation with which religious pluralism threatens the believer. Indeed, he imagines a profound degree of convergence among the world's religions in the future, so that the differences among traditions such as Hinduism, Buddhism, Judaism, Islam, and Christianity come to be seen as akin to the relatively mild differences that exist among so-called Christian "denominations" today.[16]

What is more, the suggestion that perhaps the elements of immanence and experience are more applicable to the founders of religions in Hick's view than to their workaday followers raises an additional issue that ought at least to be mentioned here. If there is such a thing as an "average" believer – not to be confused with our ideal type of the traditional Christian, the individual who is on the quest of faith seeking understanding and thus is anything but average – say, an average Christian who finds himself or herself sitting in church on most Sunday mornings, isn't it likely that this person's sense of divine immanence and experience of the divine, including its ineffability, will most likely all be fairly mild? Our hypothetical average Christian will indeed have the experience of feeling closer to God in church than he or she does while at the office during the work week, but the sense of immanence and its accompanying experience will probably be less dramatic than what writers such as Thich Nhat Hahn, Deepak Chopra, and John Shelby Spong describe. The upshot of this is that the seeker who goes to the trouble of adopting a modification strategy because that seeker is troubled by the disconfirming Other is, generally speaking, more intensely involved in the spiritual life than most. It is these latter persons, in other words, whose sense of immanence and personal experience of the divine may be characterized by the intensity suggested in the thinking of Nhat Hahn, Chopra, and Spong.

Pluralism has been at the heart of our entire investigation up to this point. Specifically, we have been interested in how religious persons deal with the threat of disconfirmation that spiritual pluralism wields. When it comes to modification strategies that attempt to face that threat head-on, we have seen how those strategies rely upon immanence, experience, and ineffability as essential motifs. A bit of further investigation, however, will reveal that two of these all-important motifs have a circular relationship with pluralism. More exactly, they exist in a reciprocal causal relationship with pluralism. We shall begin with the paradoxical fact that an emphasis upon immanence and experience, which the modification strategies use as tools for warding off the threatening aspect of pluralism, is itself the product of American society's spiritual pluralism. Then we shall consider how the modification strategies add to that same pluralism.

How is it that writers such as Thich Nhat Hahn, Deepak Chopra, and John Shelby Spong can so effectively appeal to the notion that the ultimate is immanent and that spirituality is built around individual experience? They can do so, at least where their American audiences are concerned, because, as we have seen, these notions are already firmly ensconced in American culture. As Harold Bloom has suggested, the American spiritual seeker believes that the soul is older than creation. It is always already intimately tied up with ultimate reality. But the nearly taken-for-granted status of divine immanence and immediate experiential access to divinity in America is the result of spiritual pluralism. In noting the ready-to-hand character of these motifs in America we have cited the importance of figures such as Ralph Waldo Emerson. We need to remind ourselves that historically influential American spiritual questers who emphasized immanence and individual spiritual experience such as Emerson and his fellow-travelers, from Mary Baker Eddy to Madame Blavatsky, are potent examples of American spiritual pluralism. That is, the historically most effective spokespersons in this country for immanence and experience in the life of the spirit frequently stood outside the walls of mainstream religion and contributed decisively to the diversity of American spiritualities.

Of course, divine immanence has ever been one pole of the traditional Christian dialectic of immanence and transcendence, and we recall that revivalism and Christian fundamentalism both put a premium on an emotionally-charged experience of Jesus Christ as their savior. But the emphasis on immanence and the closely-connected notion of individual experience of divinity are taken much further by Emerson and his ilk than most orthodox Christians would be willing to go. One need only think here about traditional Christianity's opposition to the notion of private revelations. That is, traditional church theology, both Catholic and Protestant, has held that, while the individual believer can feel God's presence and be guided by God in making decisions, no insight into the divine nature itself that is not already a part of the orthodox deposit of revelation will ever be vouchsafed an individual, a principle that Emerson clearly transgresses. Recall that this was, in fact, one of the sticking points between Martin Luther and the so-called "radical reformers." For Luther, radical reformers such as Andreas Karlstadt went far too far in allowing for the possibility that God can speak directly to the individual believer. Hence, Luther's famous dismissive observation that Karlstadt had "swallowed the Holy Spirit, feathers and all."

Note that the tie to pluralism here is not only a function of the fact that the movers and shakers in American history who put special emphasis upon immanence and individual spiritual experience frequently stood outside the religious mainstream. It is also the case that those favored themes of divine immanence and the individual's experiential access to divinity are themselves inextricably tied up with pluralism, for they empower the individual quester to follow an idiosyncratic spiritual path, thus encouraging the creation of a multitude of unique spiritualities. Hence, we find that the very motifs employed by the modification strategies to block pluralism's potential threat to belief are themselves (before they are taken up into the modification strategies) a result of and even productive of America's history of vigorous spiritual pluralism.

But the modification strategies that have been under investigation here not only encourage a variety of faiths in the sense that they privilege the divine presence within each individual and each individual's experience of the divine: they also encourage further pluralism in that they offer the possibility of any number of different combinations of exemplars of the ultimate. For instance, Thich Nhat Hahn is explicit about his having grafted the figure of Jesus onto his already existing reverence for the Buddha. But others are free to privilege Jesus and the Quran, or Jesus and Krishna, or Jesus and the Tao, and on and on. Thus it is that the modification strategies, in countering the threat of disconfirmation represented by spiritual pluralism, draw constituent elements from that same spiritual pluralism and even contribute to its expansion.

That the modification strategies draw upon and even enhance that spiritual pluralism the disconfirming power of which they are meant to parry suggests a circular, reciprocal causal pattern. But is this circle vicious and destructive? Thich Nhat Hahn and Deepak Chopra suggested that belief in Jesus as the presence of God is consistent with Buddhism and with much of what goes under the heading of Hinduism, and Spong implied as much. And if commitment to Jesus is consistent with these, it surely ought potentially to be consistent with Christianity's sister religions, Judaism and Islam. The suggestion, in other words, is that the modification strategies can disarm pluralism's threat of disconfirmation when the pluralism in question is that of the major world religions. Thich Nhat Hahn and Deepak Chopra, in particular, suggested that this was the case by grappling with specific tenets of Christianity, Hinduism, and Buddhism. They did not grapple, however, with specific tenets of the endless number of smaller spiritual movements, from ancient preliterate traditions to Zoroastrianism to Scientology. No doubt it is most often the other great world religions that a believer finds most challenging: reflective Christians are troubled by the fact that their convictions appear, on the surface, to be contradicted by the other world religions and that they have no stronger basis for their convictions than do the adherents of those other world religions. By contrast, they may lose little sleep over their lack of any definitive epistemological edge over Scientology. But is this untroubled slumber justified?

The arguments set forth by Nhat Hahn, Chopra, and indirectly by Spong, as well as the position staked out by Rahner, did not aver that, simply as a function of mere chance, there are profound, underlying similarities among the world religions. Rather, they engaged in theological or spiritual anthropology: they analyzed the human way of being and the quest for the ultimate that follows from it, and they found certain features that they hold to be universal. It is part of being human to have a relationship to the ultimate or infinite in which the latter is potentially immanent in the former; it is part of the human way of being to be able to connect with this infinite or ultimate via a particular kind of experience; and the spiritual experiences that we have, as well as the reality to which they point, are often ineffable. Undeterred by postmodernist strictures against the notion of human nature, the thinkers we have profiled did attempt to describe the universal human condition, and they found the relevant forms of immanence, experience, and ineffability at its heart.

As a result, the Christian believer who is willing to modify the orthodox outlines of his or her belief system can regard adherence to the figure of Jesus Christ as perfectly consistent with what is going on in the other world religions; there are no contradictions after all and, hence, no problem with the fact that those other traditions too appeal to phenomena such as divine revelation to back up their claims. If the Christian believer, having adopted the sort of modification strategies we have been investigating here, can feel at home among the other world religions rather than in danger of being undone by them as competing belief systems, a great deal has been accomplished indeed. Far from a confrontation with the other world religions sowing seeds of doubt about one's own convictions, the underlying unity among them, based on the universal phenomena represented by immanence, experience, and ineffability, obviously enhances the plausibility structure undergirding those convictions: there is strength in numbers.

So what, then, if traditions such as Scientology, without the worldwide impact of those commonly regarded as the great world religions, do not share the emphases upon immanence, experience, and ineffability found in the most venerable world religions? Does the specter of the disconfirming Other now simply arise from new quarters? It need not. Not only does the now-apparent underlying agreement among the vast majority of spiritual questers in the world, the members of the world religions, provide a potent plausibility structure that may well allow the Christian simply to disregard hundreds of smaller spiritual movements that may still contradict his or her convictions: that Christian (or Buddhist, or Hindu, or other devotee of a world religion) can disregard them in good conscience precisely because, as contradictory, these movements must be assumed not to be putting proper emphasis upon the unifying motifs of immanence, experience, and ineffability.

The worldview pushed by writers such as Nhat Hahn and Chopra asserts, as we have seen, that these motifs are built into the nature of human being. Hence, for a smaller movement such as Scientology to contradict my own convictions by underplaying immanence, experience, and ineffability is a function of it failing accurately to read the human condition. In other words, in contrast to where the believer found herself when first confronted with the potentially disconfirming power of the Other, that believer now possesses clear convictions about how immanence, experience, and ineffability inform her beliefs and about their presence within the other world religions, and thus, this time around, the believer does in fact possess criteria that ground her convictions, criteria that are presumably lacking in spiritual movements that contradict those convictions.[17]

This is not the last word on spiritual and religious pluralism, however, nor even upon their potentially destructive effects. For we have yet to examine a portion of American spirituality where pluralism might be said to run wild, and where anything resembling the traditional world religions is conspicuously absent: it is time for us to turn to an investigation of New Age spirituality.

CHAPTER FIVE

Pluralism and the New Age

What is loosely designated "New Age spirituality" in America today clearly has its roots in what Catherine Albanese calls "metaphysical religion."[1] Recall the four defining characteristics of metaphysical religion that she provides. First, it focuses upon mind and its powers, where mind is an expansive concept leading all the way to psychic notions such as clairvoyance. Second, it emphasizes a correspondence between a divine macrocosm and the human microcosm (an emphasis consistent with Harold Bloom's contention that characteristically American religion regards the soul as older than creation: the soul essentially is the divine in microcosm). Third, metaphysical religion's approach to reality emphasizes movement and energy. And fourth, the metaphysical quest seeks therapeutic effects for the agitated human soul.

If so-called New Age spirituality is a contemporary manifestation of this metaphysical spirituality, with metaphysical spirituality having been a part of nearly the whole of American history, what distinguishes the New Age from the rest of that history? Albanese suggests that the "New Age movement" came into being sometime in the 1970s and 1980s when a critical mass of metaphysical practitioners became aware of their own impressive numbers and when, as a result, both the practitioners and the press became convinced that they could identify a genuine, discreet spiritual movement in American culture.[2]

A perusal of the New Age section of a typical bookstore or of an internet bookseller's New Age offerings will inevitably reveal the following topics, among others: astrology, Tarot, the *I-Ching*, channeling the dead (that is, communicating with the dead via a "medium"), the body's *chakras* or energy centers, aroma therapy, healing through the manipulation of energy fields (Reiki, for example), the meaning of dreams, extra-sensory perception, the power of crystals, palmistry, casting spells, Native-American spirituality, eco-spirituality, past lives regression therapy (where one is aided in recalling one's previous incarnations on the wheel of rebirth), and devotion to the Goddess or goddesses. This list, though inevitably incomplete, makes it clear that the New Age is the pluralistic spirituality *par excellence*. But its pluralism is not simply a function of how many practices it offers its devotees – the plethora of the sources upon which it draws – but also of the fact that the individual New Age practitioner is free to take up as many of these practices as he or she sees fit. In other words, the pluralism of the sources of New Age spirituality is coupled with what might be called an internal pluralism: a quester is likely to experiment not just with one offering collected under the New Age heading but, rather, an array of practices that suits his or her individual needs.

Our interest in pluralism in this study, however, has been with its potentially disconfirming powers. More specifically, we have considered how a reasonably orthodox adherent of one of the great world religions deals with the fact that the other world religions profess beliefs contrary to her own, and that she recognizes the fact that she has no more evidence to back up her beliefs than members of other religions have to support theirs. The latter part of this formula is crucial: the Christian will claim divine revelation as a source of his beliefs, but the Muslim will also claim divine revelation as the source of her convictions. Note, however, that this second component of the disconfirmation dilemma probably will not come into play when the New Age believer confronts the traditional world religions. The devotee of the New Age will, in most cases, not appeal to divine revelation contained in a sacred Scripture, for example, which is something that at least the three Abrahamic religions certainly will. The matter is more ambiguous when we attempt to compare New Age claims about sources of truth with something such as the claim made on behalf of the Upanishads, namely, that their content was intuited by special seers. Because we are concentrating upon spirituality and religion in the United States, however, it is most pertinent, for our purposes, to think about how New Age spirituality lines up with the Abrahamic traditions, Judaism and Christianity in particular. And to the extent that the New Age mentality will make appeal to very different sources of evidence than do Judaism and Christianity, the New Age believer is not as likely to be confronted with the threat of disconfirmation from those traditions. For, given that the New Age sources are genuinely different than those claimed by the Abrahamic traditions, the devotee of the New Age can always claim that the basis for New Age convictions is more profound and reliable than what props up the beliefs of Jews and Christians.

The very idea of a "new age," after all, suggests that we can tap into a new spiritual dispensation, one unavailable to, or at least unrecognized by, the traditional world religions. Recalling Albanese's four characteristics of metaphysical religion and condensing them into a summary formula that can be used to describe just what New Age practitioners see as the source of New Age rites, we can say that they claim that a potent energy fills the universe and that enlightened human beings can tap into it and experience first-hand its therapeutic effects. They can do so since all humans are from the start, whether or not they are sufficiently enlightened to recognize it, connected to this supernal energy; the soul, once more, is older than creation. Our conclusion, then, is that a self-described New Age spiritual seeker will not confront the disconfirming Other when considering the beliefs of Christianity or Judaism, for that quester will inevitably point out that those older religious traditions simply do not afford the New Age's much more immediate relation to the energy that fructifies the universe.

But we have seen that New Age spirituality is tied up with American spiritual pluralism not only in the vast array of spiritual traditions (traditions most often outside Judaism and Christianity) upon which it draws, but that that spirituality is inevitably internally pluralistic as well. Might not the problem of the disconfirming Other arise here, since now we are not juxtaposing the New Age with Christianity or Judaism, but, rather, considering persons who all fit under the New Age umbrella that we have described above? What we appear to have in many instances of what gets labeled New Age spirituality is a whole host of spiritual practices that differ in their specifics yet all rest upon a worldview according to which the properly prepared mind (and body) can participate in some type of encompassing, therapeutic energy field, whether that field is most easily accessed by reading the stars or by manipulating the body's own chakras. Now we seem to have the necessary ingredients for a disconfirmation challenge: my New Age practices will differ from those of some other practitioners and may seem to contradict those other practices, yet my defense of the efficacy of my practices – the ability of the enlightened mind to tap into healing energy – will be little different from that advanced by those engaging in practices apparently incommensurable with my own. Suppose I look to a medium and communication with the dead in order to see into the future, while you do not believe in such "channeling" and turn instead to casting the *I-Ching* or look to a psychic who claims no connection with the departed. Aren't we now right back where we started, namely, with Charles Taylor's "mutual fragilization" of belief, the challenge of the disconfirming Other?

One clue that the answer to this question may be "No" is to be found in our description of New Age spirituality as being internally pluralistic, meaning not just that many different practices can go on under one big conceptual tent, but that the individual New Ager, *qua* individual, frequently adopts a multitude of spiritual practices, practices which may appear to an outsider to be mutually exclusive. One finds empirical evidence of this by, for example, attending one of the Celebrate Your Life conferences that have been held for several years across the United States, where one finds seekers enthusiastically participating in a menagerie of New Age events. Of course, we might choose to argue that the practices do in fact often rest on contradictory notions that become apparent when we push beyond the superficial New Age similarities (the notion of energy fields and the like) and that therefore we ought to conclude that

New Age practitioners are employing one or more of the avoidance tactics that we explored in Chapter One – compartmentalization, overstepping the bounds of logic, and self-deception – in order to ward off disconfirmation. But this would, I think, be an overly hasty conclusion, for the ease with which an individual New Age devotee is able to pull together a conglomeration of different spiritual practices suggests that there are dynamics at work in the New Age mentality that are simply not ordinarily a part of the mainline religions.

It turns out that there are at least two important answers to the question "How is the New Age devotee protected from disconfirmation given that he or she is allowed, if not encouraged, to adopt a potpourri of New Age practices?" The answers are not independent of one another, but fit together into a coherent New Age package. First of all, one should note that the list of New Age options proffered above is not, first and foremost, a conglomeration of different belief-systems. It is, rather, more akin to a list of different *techniques.* If we were to compare these options to what goes on in the Christian tradition, we would have to conclude that they are more akin to intercessory prayer than to reciting the Apostle's Creed. And while it would be foolish not to recognize that some persons are attracted to metaphysical and New Age spiritualities precisely because of the speculative worldviews that they offer – some devotees of theosophy might fit in this category, for example – the New Age is above all a therapeutic approach to the human condition and its sundry challenges, an approach meant in a very direct sense to help you through the practical challenges of life and to cure what ails you, whether your ailments be physical, psychological, or left over from a previous life. And just as there may be several treatment options open to a decidedly non-New Age physician in treating a patient's illness, so the New Age offers a host of techniques that, while they may appear to contradict one another when mistakenly understood as essentially belief systems, avoid contradiction when understood as techniques. Different belief systems or worldviews conflict; different practical techniques need not.[3]

Second, it is hard to miss the element of commodification in New Age spirituality. I can personally testify that a visit to a New Age convention, such as the aforementioned Celebrate Your Life events, affords one the opportunity to walk up and down the aisles of an exhibition hall with its myriad books, DVDs, and other New Age wares in almost the same way that one goes up and down the aisles at the supermarket: I see many things in the supermarket that I don't care to eat, but that does not bother me in the least, for there will also be a whole host of foods that I do like to eat. As long as my nutritional needs and desires are met by my supermarket, I have no reason to begrudge others access to foods that are to their taste but not to mine. In other words, I am expected to "shop," not just in the literal sense that occurs at a New Age convention, but to shop also among different spiritual techniques by trying them out in my quest.

These two considerations fit together nicely: techniques offer themselves up for commodification in a way that worldviews do not. One does actually pay for a session with a medium or a treatment intended to put one's energy centers back in balance. By contrast, while the traditional mainline church attendee may put money in the collection plate on most Sunday mornings, this is hardly a matter of directly purchasing the belief system proclaimed in that church.

It is essential to note, however, that while the New Age emphasis on technique and commodification means that the New Age is, with the inevitable exceptions noted above, less invested in belief-systems than many other forms of spirituality, the belief system dimension cannot easily disappear altogether for *any* New Age practitioner, but is simply relegated to second-tier status. We have already mentioned the general New Age conviction about access to special forms of cosmic energy. Furthermore, the techniques that the New Age sells its devotees, from astrology to channeling the dead, each presuppose certain more specific convictions. Astrology, for example, clearly commits one to the belief that the stars have a powerful connection with the fates of individual human beings. And in order to buy into the notion of channeling the deceased, one must believe that there is some form of life after death and that the dead are sufficiently interested in those of us here below that they are willing to provide us with guidance.

Yet, the mixing and matching of individual spiritual practices that characterizes the life of the New Age seeker suggests that the belief systems behind the practices do not ordinarily conflict with one another to the point of disconfirmation. Perhaps they can, after all, work together smoothly under the overarching belief that enlightened human beings can tap into special sources of spiritual energy. But this does not protect New Age spirituality from disconfirmation. For the New Age's investment in technique brings to the fore a different kind of disconfirmation threat: the claim that a particular technique provides physical healing or allows one to make accurate predictions about the future can be empirically tested.

Let us consider a concrete example, one connected to one of the New Age's most audacious claims, namely, that certain persons dubbed mediums have the ability to contact the dead and to receive various sorts of information from them, including information about events that will occur in the future. Two of America's currently most famous mediums are John Edward and James Van Praagh. They appear regularly on U.S. television, and they have sold millions of copies of their many books. Most often these alleged mediums are seen not working with simply one inquirer (though one can pay to have such one-on-one sessions) but with a whole room full. One would expect skeptics, especially those with the training to engage in statistical analysis, to have challenged the claims of alleged mediums, and indeed they have.

Mediums such as Edward and Van Praagh frequently begin a session by asking their audience a question such as "Does the name Eddie mean anything to anyone here? I am getting a very strong impression connected with that name." In any group of twenty people or more – and mediums such as Van Praagh and Edward usually work with significantly larger groups – there is bound to be someone who is named Eddie or who at least knows someone of that name. Where the latter category is concerned, someone in the audience will inevitably say that they had a dog named Eddie or that their second cousin is named Eddie; some person in the audience will find a connection with the name, however tangential. Suppose, for instance, that an audience member volunteers that she had an uncle named Eddie. Now the medium is on his or her way. He or she will ask questions of the particular person now in the spotlight, questions such as "Was Eddie ever injured in any way?" "Did Eddie have a dark complexion?" "Did Eddie's job have something to do with the business world?"

It turns out that the answers to the medium's questions will more often be negative than positive, but inquirers are apparently impressed by even a very low number of "hits" (sometimes no more than ten percent), no doubt because, as has been suggested by skeptical analysts, these inquirers so desperately want to connect with a deceased loved one. Skeptics have actually gone so far as to pretend to be mediums and have demonstrated that by carefully listening to the responses they get from their inquirers, they can come up with as much or more accurate information than the alleged mediums do.[4]

Of course, channeling the dead does not constitute the whole of the New Age. For example, many New Age techniques are invoked for physical healing. In some cases, the claim will be that a gifted New Age practitioner can directly heal an ill person by manipulating the patient's energy fields. In other instances one consults a New Age shaman who claims to be schooled in so-called "alternative" treatments and in the therapeutic use of various substances, the farther outside the scope of traditional scientific medical practice in the United States the better. It will come as no great surprise to those outside New Age circles, however, that, when rigorous tests are performed to assess the sorts of alternative therapies that are now so popular among New Age practitioners, here too the claims cannot be verified.[5]

Long before there was a movement known as the New Age, there has been an intense interest in America in claims about "psychic phenomena," involving everything from telepathy to the existence of ghosts to the mind's ability to manipulate matter at a distance. What is more, there have been, and continue to be, a whole host of institutes and "research centers" dedicated to investigating psychic claims and trumpeting positive results from their inquiries. The Edgar Cayce Institute is a good example, named after one of the country's most famous twentieth-century claimants to psychic abilities. But, alas, once again, when science of the most rigorous kind puts the claims of the psychics to the test, those claims almost invariably prove thoroughly unfounded. The experience of psychologist Susan Blackmore, who began her Ph.D. studies convinced of the reality of psychic phenomena, is instructive in this regard:

> I did the experiments. I tested telepathy, precognition, and clairvoyance; I got only chance results. I trained fellow students in imagery techniques and tested them again; chance results. I tested twins in pairs; chance results. I worked in play groups and nursery schools with very young children (their naturally telepathic minds are not yet warped by education, you see); chance results. I trained as a Tarot reader and tested the readings; chance results.
>
> Occasionally I got a significant result. Oh, the excitement! I responded as I think any scientist should, by checking for errors, recalculating the statistics, and repeating the experiments. But every time I either found the error responsible, or failed to repeat the results.[6]

Blackmore tells us that "parapsychologists called me a 'psi-inhibitory experimenter,' meaning that I didn't get paranormal results because I didn't believe strongly enough. I studied other people's results and found more errors, and even outright fraud."[7]

I have suggested that the belief-system component of spirituality takes a back seat to technique and commodification in New Age spirituality. And we have seen how this emphasis on technique and commodity and the relegation of a belief system to second-tier status protects the New Age devotee from the kind of disconfirmation with which we have been concerned in previous chapters of this book, namely, disconfirmation via the other believer. We have gone on to note, however, that New Age claims about techniques face their own kind of disconfirmation challenge: precisely as clearly delimited claims about specific phenomena that New Age spirituality can effect, New Age contentions leave themselves open to scientific falsification, or at least to the scientific conclusion that there is no tangible evidence to back up New Age contentions.

This state of affairs leads to two pertinent observations. First, while there seems to be less emphasis on commodified techniques among the world religions and more emphasis upon a religion as a belief system, those traditional religions do sometimes venture into territory that seems to parallel New Age claims regarding techniques. For instance, Christians of some stripes put a great deal of emphasis upon petitionary prayer, that is, prayer in which they ask God to accomplish some particular feat, such as healing a diseased loved one. Cannot one scientifically test the Christian claim that God responds to prayer and heals the sick in much the same fashion as one can test New Age claims (and find them wanting)? As a matter of fact, one can indeed do so, and the most rigorous tests done thus far on petitionary prayer for the ill have turned up largely negative results. Ill persons being prayed for showed no more improvement in their health than did control groups for whom no prayers were said.[8]

But the notion of petitionary prayer is embedded in a complex fashion within Christianity as a belief system such that the believer can fairly easily deal with such negative evidence from scientific tests of the efficacy of prayer. For example, the believer will trust that God has very good reasons for not answering some prayers. Perhaps a particular bout of illness that befalls John fits into God's overarching plan for John's life and will ultimately serve a good end. Or consider the fact that there is biblical precedent for not "putting God to the test" (Deuteronomy 6:16). Hence, the believer may conclude that while, under ordinary circumstances, petitionary prayer can have miraculous consequences, a controlled study testing prayer is not a project in which the Almighty chooses to participate.

The second observation resulting from the New Age's susceptibility to scientific testing of its techniques is to note that, interestingly enough, some New Age commentators have fought back by reversing the decision to place the intellectual or belief-system component of their spirituality in the background: they have attempted to articulate a detailed explanation of what Albanese has pointed to as metaphysical spirituality's perennial reference to movement and energy. The thinking here is of the "If-you-can't-beat-them-join-them" variety. That is, numerous New Age thinkers have attempted, in essence, to protect New Age practice from scientific disconfirmation by arguing that the very latest scientific discoveries about the human mind, energy, and the place each holds in the structure of the universe actually support New Age claims.

The most fertile ground among the sciences for such New Age counterattacks is quantum physics, with its notoriously mind-bending claims about the counter-intuitive way the universe works on the most microscopic of levels. In her book *The Field: The Quest for the Secret Force of the Universe*, New Age author Lynne McTaggart focuses on the energy fluctuations that quantum physicists talk about as existing in what they call the quantum field. For her, the quantum physicists' failings are in not going beyond the purely scientific implications of their discoveries and neglecting the metaphysical implications. If one does the latter, which she sets out to do in her book, some of the most fantastic of New Age claims supposedly become plausible, including its all-important claims about alternative methods for healing: "The field is the force, rather than germs or genes, that finally determines whether we are healthy or ill, the force which must be tapped in order to heal."[9]

To take a second example, the writing team of Phaedra and Isaac Bonewits claims in their book *Real Energy: Systems, Spirits, and Substances to Heal, Change, and Grow* that the genuinely astute student of the universe's energy can seamlessly combine energy as understood in contemporary physics with Ceremonial Magic, Voodoo and Santeria, Taoism, t'ai chi, tantra and kundalini yoga.[10]

If there is one overarching and overawing assertion made by those who claim quantum scientific backing for New Age beliefs, it is probably, as Victor Stenger has suggested, that it is our own thinking that creates reality.[11] This is, after all, the central notion, in one of its many permutations, behind the hugely popular book, *The Secret*, and it is trumpeted throughout the surprisingly successful New Age film, *What the Bleep Do We Know?* (which is particularly strenuous in claiming quantum physics on behalf of the New Age).[12]

Here is the strategy, then: argue that the familiar scientific tests of New Age claims, such as those undertaken by Susan Blackmore, are not tuned into the newest and most profound scientific discoveries, that is, those found in quantum physics. If quantum physics is understood aright, then New Age claims suddenly become plausible, even intellectually respectable. After all, there is no more prestigious claimant to the title of intellectual arbiter in contemporary Western culture than the scientist. The problem, of course, is that this New Age strategy falls flat if the vast majority of quantum physicists dismiss it as a wild misreading of their field, which is in fact what has happened. New Age talk of quantum physics is what Michael Shermer, with a nod to Nobel laureate Murray Gell Mann, has dubbed "quantum flapdoodle and other flummery."[13]

At this point, it behooves us to step back and regain the big picture, lest we lose the proverbial forest, our central concern in this investigation, for the equally proverbial trees. Let us look back over what we have found. What, precisely, is the relation of New Age spirituality to pluralism? The New Age movement is wholeheartedly pluralistic in the number of different sources upon which it draws. More important, it is internally pluralistic in that it encourages individual practitioners to imbibe as many New Age products as he or she sees fit. But does not this internal pluralism, in particular, lead to a form of disconfirmation? Does not the individual New Age devotee find that the various practices that he or she tries contradict one another? Not necessarily, and we have attributed this particular instance of resistance to disconfirmation to the fact that the New Age is more about a pluralism of techniques, indeed techniques that have become, for all practical purposes, commodities for sale, as opposed to being about belief systems.

However, this emphasis upon technique and commodification opens the New Age to a different kind of disconfirmation: the individual techniques, thanks to the specificity of the claims attached to them, can be empirically tested in order to determine if they deliver what they promise. What is more, there is still a connection with pluralism in this version of the challenge of disconfirmation: pluralism does raise the threat of disconfirmation here, but not by confronting different belief systems with one another. Rather, the sheer number of practices offered by the New Age mentality – practice taking pride of place over worldview in this instance – coupled with the assumption that these many practices can be mixed and matched, tends to turn those practices into commodities. That is, in the case of the New Age, commodification is in large measure a function of offering the quester so many choices that the spiritual quest becomes essentially a shopping spree. This suggests that pluralism within the New Age, especially what we have called internal pluralism, reinforces, if it does not explain all by itself, commodification. And the commodification of New Age wares is in sync with the emphasis on technique over worldview. In summary, insofar as New Age claims are susceptible to empirical disconfirmation, and to the degree that the emphasis on technique and commodification that is largely responsible for this form of disconfirmation is tied to the New Age's thoroughgoing pluralism, the link between pluralism and the threat of disconfirmation remains, albeit in a different form than that represented by the disconfirming Other, the bane of adherents of more traditional religions.

And, alas, the attempt of some writers to rescue New Age claims from the special kind of disconfirmation to which the New Age's commodified techniques are susceptible by tying them to quantum physics or other branches of contemporary science (that is, to focus more on cognitive claims and a bit less on technique and commodity) has been, at least from the perspective of the larger scientific community itself, wholly unconvincing. One can only conclude that, where the New Age is concerned, pluralism, via its connections with commodification and the notion of New Age practice as technique, has found a way to raise the specter of disconfirmation here too. We are hardly in a position here to offer a final pronouncement, the last word, on New Age spirituality. It is indeed much too "new," on the timescale of history, for us to know where it will all end up. But in its present configuration, and given its vulnerability to disconfirmation via empirical testing, the New Age movement seems simply to offer an alternative form of pluralism-induced disconfirmation.

CHAPTER SIX

The Modification Strategies:
A Concluding Analysis

As the year 2012 dawned, the journal *The Economist* greeted its readers with the following information:

> In Nigeria scores of Christians have died in Islamist bomb attacks, targeting Christmas Prayers. In Iran and Pakistan Christians are on death row, for "apostasy" – quitting Islam – or blasphemy. Dozens of churches in Indonesia have been attacked or shut. Two-thirds of Iraq's pre-war Christian population have fled. In Egypt and Syria, where secular despots gave Christianity a shield of sorts, political upheaval and Muslim zeal threaten ancient Christian groups. Not all Christianity's woes are down to Muslims. The faith faces harassment in formally communist China and Vietnam. In India Hindu nationalists want to penalize Christians who make converts. . . . Regimes or societies that penalize Christians tend to oppress others minorities too. Sunni Muslims who demonize Christians loathe Shias.[1]

One does not often hear about violence against Christians. We hear more frequently, for instance, about the violent conflict between Hindus and Muslims in India. But this account serves to remind us that religious violence is not limited to only one or two of the world religions. Above all, it should remind us that the desire to adopt modification strategies is not simply about persons addressing abstract challenges that confront them as intellectually curious individuals: it is also about the possibility of undercutting the causes of violent persecution.

Having reminded ourselves of the serious implications of our topic, suppose that we begin this final chapter with a thought experiment. Imagine that the use of modification strategies such as those we have explored in the previous chapters becomes widespread. Two results are likely to follow. First, religious pluralism, far from being a threatening source of disconfirmation of one's beliefs, will be heralded as effecting a particular moral good (one that we first met in Chapter Three in our discussion of Karl Rahner). If the world religions were in fact inconsistent, I would face the Other as a source of disconfirmation. In addition, to the extent that I nevertheless attempted to maintain my conviction that my own belief system was correct even though it contradicted the other religious belief systems, I would likely experience the moral burden of feeling that the vast majority of my fellow inhabitants of planet Earth were being denied access to salvific truth. But the modification strategies eliminate this moral conundrum as effectively as they ward off disconfirmation: questers in other traditions are not destined to be cast into the outer darkness but are fellow travelers who will simply reach the same mountaintop via a different path.

Now those who have adopted the modification strategies and who read them as a much more sensitive moral stance toward the Other than the exclusivism with which they began will trumpet the moral responsibility to embrace their newly discovered pluralistic theology. As a result, far from being a threat that ought to be feared, religious and spiritual pluralism, specifically the particular approach to pluralism associated with the modification strategies, will be hailed as something that ought to be taken up by all sensitive souls. The duty to embrace theological pluralism will, for many, take on the impassioned character of a creed.

But in addition to taking up a pluralist theology as a moral as well as spiritual duty, champions of such a pluralist theology might reasonably be regarded as utilizing a genuinely distinctive religious or spiritual epistemology. Whereas before embracing the modification strategies, the plurality of religions in my midst weakened the plausibility structure of my own faith, now the situation is reversed: because every one of the world religions is believed to be engaged in essentially the same enterprise as I am in my faith, the plausibility of religious and spiritual belief and practice is now high. That is, the general tenets of my spiritual convictions are now mirrored, with what are essentially only cultural differences (perhaps in the manner that John Hick proposes), in the spiritual convictions of all of the other world religions so that nothing could seem more plausible than the existence of the ultimate reality to which they mutually point.

But something more results from the employment of the modification strategies allowing us justifiably to speak of a new state of affairs in religious epistemology. Specifically, widespread adoption of the notion that the Others' religions are just different routes to the same truth to which mine leads gives new life to the notion of a religious sense built into the human mind, a capacity that can intuit the presence of the ultimate in a fashion parallel to how the physical world is given to us through our five senses.

This is, of course, an entirely familiar claim among the world's pious (not to mention among various influential nineteenth-century thinkers such as the German Post-Kantians and the American Transcendentalists). But let us distinguish two varieties of this specially attuned sense. First, there are those who would claim for it the ability to receive specific truths communicated from on high, whether in the form that the Upanishads are said to be the product of specially gifted seers or in the form of heirs of the radical Reformation who claim to receive specific messages from God. The second form of the claim that human beings possess a special religious sense is more modest than the first. Rather than supposing that individual persons can receive detailed revelations from God, this version of the notion of religious intuition holds that we are put together in such a way that it is possible for us to intuit the presence of the ultimate (i.e., rather than a detailed message from that same ultimate). Rahner's claim, based on his version of transcendental method, that we all possess an unthematic and preliminary awareness of God can be seen as one form of this more modest proposal about a faculty of religious intuition (though it is well to remember that Rahner did not himself move beyond inclusivism to a full-blown pluralist theology). And it coheres with the specific sorts of claims about the role of experience and of sensing the divine presence that we encountered in our three paradigmatic authors regarding modification strategies, namely, Thich Nhat Hahn, Deepak Chopra, and John Shelby Spong. Hence it is this second, more modest form of the claim that we possess an intuitive faculty sensitive to ultimate reality that will be at issue for us here.

In a world where the widespread adoption of modification strategies has not yet occurred, not only will the encounter of the world religions lead the most honest and probing questers to fear that the existence of a multitude of other religions with other beliefs are disconfirming of their own, but the claim to an intuitive faculty aimed at the transcendent, a sense in addition to the five earth-bound senses, will appear unfounded and even falsifiable. In order to see how this is so, one need only consider how differently a physical sense such as sight operates than does an alleged sense specially attuned to the ultimate. Suppose that you and I are walking along a path in the woods at dusk. Suddenly, I stop and grab you by the shoulder in order to stop you as well. I point to a spot several hundred feet ahead of us on the trail and whisper excitedly, "There's a bear ahead!" You, however, disagree: "That's just a large tree limb that has fallen across the path." One of the constitutive aspects of our regular five senses is that their deliverances can be put to the test of inter-subjective validity. To continue our story, you bravely walk toward the disputed object on the trail before us, while I hang back in fear and trepidation. You walk right up to the thing, motion for me to follow, and shout out: "I told you: it's just an old tree limb," at which point I walk toward you, sheepishly no doubt, and as I get close, I can see for myself that what had looked to me like a bear is indeed nothing more than an old tree limb.

This not uncommon sort of incident shows that, while my five senses can deceive me or be defective in some circumstances – the senses may sometimes be undermined by something as insignificant as a poorly digested bit of dinner, as Ebenezer Scrooge avers to the ghost of Jacob Marley – most of the time I have every reason to trust that they are essentially reliable, precisely because I and my fellow human beings will, at least after a little investigation, agree about the sort of thing that, to remain with the sense of sight, we are seeing (even if we cannot figure out what the thing is, we will be able to agree on the traits it presents to our vision). The momentous problem that the claim to an intuitive religious sense faces (even when the claim is only the modest one that we can intuit the divine presence, not the more radical clam that we can receive specific revelatory content) is that, when the world religions are regarded as mutually contradictory, then we have no inter-subjective agreement to reassure us about the soundness of such a religious sense. In fact, such an intuitive faculty will appear to be nothing more than wishful thinking, given the fact that the alleged ultimate reality that my tradition claims can be intuited will inevitably be appear significantly different from the ultimate reality that your tradition claims you can intuit.

If, however, all of the world's major religions are understood to be pointing to the same ultimate reality, then I could be excused for holding that what persons from traditions other than my own are given by their religious intuition is basically the same ultimate reality that I intuit. Inter-subjective validity can now be understood as being applicable to a religious sense in essentially the same fashion as it is to the five physical senses. If one does embrace this optimistic approach toward the existence of a reliable intuitive faculty where ultimate reality is concerned, then it is perhaps not such a stretch to suppose that scientific experimentation might be able to shed some empirical light on its existence and operation, even if the natural sciences are ill equipped to detect the existence of the ultimate itself.

This brings us to the well-publicized work of Andrew Newberg and his colleagues, who believe that they have discovered the seat of spiritual intuition in the human brain and that they have at least a rudimentary grasp of how it works. Newberg's hypothesis centers upon the parietal lobe of the brain which contains what he calls the "Orientation Association Area." This portion of the brain orients me in space and helps create my awareness that my body possesses definite boundaries. It thereby helps to build up a sense of my being a unique entity distinguishable from the other entities that make up the universe. Newberg's fascinating work has included doing brain scans on Buddhist monks in deep meditation and Catholic nuns in the midst of contemplative prayer. At the height of their respective spiritual practices, individuals in both groups report losing the awareness of their own bounded, distinctive identities and being taken up into something much larger than themselves. Of course, the Buddhists may name what they are experiencing "emptiness," while the Catholic nuns will indubitably identify the larger reality with which they merge as "God." In any case, Newberg has consistently found that, at the height of their respective spiritual experiences, both the Buddhists' and the Catholics' brains show a readily observable quieting in the parietal lobe. In other words, according to Newberg, his brain scans are actually detecting the dissolution of the practitioners' sense of having a firmly bounded, separate identity. The quieting of the Orientation Association Area is the physical correlate of a potent sense of being absorbed into the ultimate.[2] Of course, whether this indubitably real sensation of self-transcendence actually involves merging with an ultimate reality is a question beyond the scope of Newberg's empirical investigation.

In summary, then, widespread adoption of the modification strategies would disarm the capacity of religions or spiritualities other than my own to threaten my beliefs with disconfirmation and to convict me of moral insensitivity. In addition to this negative function – negative in the sense that it removes threats – this widespread adoption would also have a positive function in that it would greatly enhance the plausibility structure undergirding belief in an ultimate, infinite reality. Furthermore, in a world full of persons who have adopted the modification strategies with which we have been dealing, the notion of a human intuitive faculty for knowing the ultimate would be rendered a distinct possibility.

Of course, there is no firm evidence to suggest that the practitioners of the world's great religions are rushing to adopt the modification strategies in large numbers, nor that they will do so anytime soon. The strategies could, of course, be embraced by a relatively small number of questers. We might do well to recall our discussion in Chapter One about the number of actual persons who can be expected to resemble our ideal type, the Christian quester dedicated to the task of faith seeking understanding. In the most stringent reading, that ideal type might be dubbed a Christian intellectual. What would be the result if, for example, my friend Bartholomew embraced the modification strategies but did not know anyone else personally who had also embraced them? At least initially, it appears that there is nothing preventing Bartholomew from making this move, though it will not have the aura of plausibility conferred upon it that it would if a large number of people, many of whom Bartholomew knew quite well, had already made the same move.[3] Yet, it would still ward off the threat of the disconfirming Other for Bartholomew, because in his own heart of hearts, he would now believe that what the Other believes does not contradict his own faith convictions.

Still, it must be admitted that to embrace the modification strategies in total isolation from the persons around me would have its challenges. The plausibility structure backing up the modification strategies would be less potent and reassuring in this scenario. And surely it will be difficult for a lone quester to embrace the modification strategies, or something like them, if religious persons around him not only fail to embrace those strategies but actually choose to emphasize the difference between their own religion and other traditions. For instance, when one major task that a religion accomplishes for its adherents is to provide them with a unique history and identity in the midst of a larger world that seeks constantly to undermine their sense of identity – some commentators interpret fundamentalist Islam, for example, in these terms – then it is understandable when that tradition self-consciously and vocally opposes something such as the notion of religious unity championed by the modification strategies. And thanks to this vehement opposition toward a theology of religious unity, Bartholomew's relatively isolated attempt to embrace the modification strategies and convince himself of the ultimate unity of the world religions will no doubt be an uphill battle compared to the task faced by those who live in a world where the modification strategies are embraced by large numbers of devotees of each of the world's major religions.

An even more sober assessment of the modification strategies and their future results from recognizing that undesirable consequences for faith might also result if modification strategies were ever widely embraced. Such unhappy consequences, if they were to materialize, would mean that religious and spiritual pluralism are, consistent with this book's title, destructive of belief after all. What, specifically, might the undesirable consequences turn out to be? First, it is not entirely implausible that adoption of the sort of modification strategies that we explored in Chapters Three and Four would cause many believers to abandon their traditional church communities.

Consider the following scenario: One begins as the sort of believer that we specified as an ideal type in Chapter One. That sort of believer was an intellectually astute Christian who could in good conscience and with a reasonable grasp of its meaning stand up in church to recite the Apostle's Creed. However, when this believer honestly confronts the threat of the disconfirming Other, she feels the need to modify her religious stance; she adopts something along the lines of the modification strategies explored above, with their emphases on immanence, experience, and ineffability. Suppose that this modified way of understanding her Christian faith provides a thoroughly satisfying spirituality for our believer. She happily embraces it and, as a result, the religious Other turns from being a potential source of disconfirmation to being a fellow traveler who reinforces the confidence of our believer in her (modified) Christian convictions.

The question at hand is whether this idealized believer will be motivated by the modification experience to cease actively participating in her church community. On the one hand, there is no necessity for her doing so, for now her Christian faith is immune from disconfirmation from the religious Other. As a result, she can be an even more confident believer and remain in her Christian church. On the other hand, her remaining in her church may require something akin to a constant, and perhaps unpalatably laborious, translation of much that she hears in worship. She will hear, for example, the famous passage from John's Gospel which quotes Jesus as saying "I am the way, the truth, and the life. No one comes to the Father except by me" (John 14:6). Having adopted a modification strategy, our ideal believer will think of this statement as requiring creative reinterpretation. Rather than taking it at face value, she may, for instance, interpret it to mean that no one can attain unity with God without enhancing his or her God-consciousness – this is Jesus' central function – but that "Jesus" here stands not just for Jesus of Nazareth but for any of the world religions' central figures.

But she may also find that such exclusivist claims, biblical or otherwise, simply go too clearly against the grain of her present religious worldview. She may now feel an outsider to her previous religious home, an outsider who no longer experiences a sense of spiritual sustenance when she attends her church. Of course, one might ask why our hypothetical believer's abandonment of her church community is necessarily undesirable. What is the problem with hitherto faithful members of churches becoming what one might call religious "free agents"? At least one answer is that through the bulk of human history, the phenomenon of community has been one of the most important assets of spirituality and religion. The ability to count on the support, both cognitive and emotional, of one's fellow believers no matter what difficulties the world throws one's way is a powerful resource in the search for a life of meaning and purpose. Such meaning and purpose can only be found if one feels reasonably secure in his or her world, and a spiritual community can go a long way indeed toward engendering that sense of security. Furthermore, at least in some brands of Christian theology, participation in the being of Christ, what Paul Tillich called the "New Being" in Jesus as the

Christ, can only be had by participation in Christ's earthly, physical body, which in the present day and age is, in essence, the Christian community, the church.[4]

Consider a second possible problem exacerbated, if not uniquely caused, by the adoption of the modification strategies we have discussed: the erstwhile member of a church may choose to abandon the form of spirituality found in that church in favor of the New Age variety. After all, once one has come to the momentous conclusion that Jesus Christ is just one way among many to unity with the ultimate, it is but a small step to buy into the New Age's estimate of spiritual beliefs and practices as just so many techniques and commodities. In that case, the question about possible disconfirmation from the Other does not even arise (at least not where other New Agers are concerned, though it may well face contradiction from mainline religions, a paradoxical situation for one who initially embraced the modification strategies precisely because of the other world religions that seemed to contradict his or her own). The disconfirmation threat fails even to arise mainly because the mindset that focuses upon technique and commodification is unlikely to raise the truth question about spiritual and religious beliefs. At the very least, as we saw in Chapter Five, New Age spirituality marginalizes the truth question. This is a decidedly undesirable outcome if one assumes, as I have assumed throughout our discussion, that truth claims are part and parcel of spiritual pursuits and that those truth claims face various challenges, including the disconfirming Other, that must be faced if one's spirituality is to maintain its integrity.

To put this problem a bit differently, the ideal type – in this case a Christian ideal type – that I sketched out at the beginning of this study and to which I have remained tied throughout the book fits the orientation of the theologian and the philosopher of religion. That is, we are focusing on those members of the Christian community – and perhaps they are decidedly in the minority – who put a good deal of emphasis upon the cognitive dimension of religion, the dimension of explicit belief, and who recognize the need to back up their truth claims with some sort of reasoning process. We have just considered the likelihood that some of these folks may be directed to the New Age camp precisely by having first confronted the modification strategies, a move that I would denigrate as having started in a position that offers rational justification for one's beliefs but ending up in a position where that intellectual rigor has been essentially abandoned. But we should take the time here to consider the fact that things could be worse. It may be that the influence of New Age spirituality and of various other *laudable* factors that push Americans toward toleration of the Other will bring many Christians into the New Age camp without any particular process of rational deliberation at all: they will *not* be induced to embrace the essentially non-rational aspects of New Age spirituality *as the paradoxical outcome of having worked through the rational modification strategies* at the heart of our deliberations. Instead, they will simply bypass the deliberation that makes up the modification strategies and, perhaps mainly due to the apparent ubiquity and emotional appeal of New Age attitudes in contemporary America, come up with what is essentially an accidental concatenation of Christian and New Age belief. Note that the persons we are imagining here are not the thoroughgoing New Agers who give up any ties to mainline religions, if ever they had such ties, or who disdain those religions. Rather, these are folks who continue to think of themselves as part of the Christian religion but who haphazardly add New Age convictions and practices to their Christianity.

That this dynamic is in fact unfolding before our eyes in the present historical moment is given empirical support by another of the Pew Charitable Trust's polls on religion (recall the polling data they provided us in the Introduction in our discussion of potential weak spots in American piety). In a poll released at the end of 2009, the Pew researchers found that 29% of those in America who identify themselves as Christian claimed to have been in touch with the dead; 17% claimed to have seen or been in the presence of ghosts; 14% consulted a psychic; 23% believed that there is spiritual energy in natural entities such as trees; 23% believed in reincarnation; and 17% believed that there is such a thing as the

Evil Eye, in other words, that some persons can place curses upon others.[5] To wax editorial for a moment, to embrace belief in the Evil Eye, and most of the other things the Pew poll lists, seems predicated on the total abandonment of interest in rigorous rationality, indeed the abandonment of the project dear to the heart of our ideal type, namely, the enterprise of "faith seeking understanding."

Of course, if we are honestly and fairly to evaluate the role of rationality in forming our spiritual convictions, we must admit a potential weak spot where rationality is concerned in the modification strategies too, whatever laudable degree of faith seeking understanding they represent. A thoughtful analysis of the modification strategies reveals that, while they can ward off the disconfirming Other, *those strategies provide no evidence at all of their own truth*. Thinking of the Christian God and of Jesus Christ in terms such as those suggested by Nhat Hahn, Chopra, and Spong may allow me to avoid anxiety about disconfirmation or about moral insensitivity, but what leads me to suppose that my new spiritual worldview accurately depicts the real ultimate and its actual relation to human life?

It is understandable that I will be inclined to accept the truth claims of a pluralist theology for the pragmatic reason that it takes care of the aforementioned anxieties: this may well make the pluralist perspective seem almost inevitably true. But while thinkers such as Nhat Hahn, Chopra, and Spong may be able to put together theological proposals that, if embraced, make the world religions largely intellectually consistent with one another and accepting of each other's salvific power, none of these admittedly significant boons of a pluralist theology provide direct evidence regarding the truth question. Simply because a theological perspective is morally sensitive and intellectually consistent does not imply that the sort of God or ultimate that the perspective presents is real. This should become all the clearer when one stops to think about the fact that different sorts of modification strategies than the ones we have investigated could no doubt also be crafted. That is, it seems theoretically possible that we could attain moral sensitivity toward and intellectual consistency among the world religions through strategies built not upon immanence, experience, and ineffability but upon completely different elements, elements that might be more salient in other cultural times and places. This would provide us with a picture of the divine that might very well conflict in various ways with the picture provided by our exploration of Nhat Hahn, Chopra, and Spong. There is simply no guarantee of truth provided by disarming the disconfirming power of the Other – though this of course eliminates one reason for thinking that one's beliefs are untrue – or by committing oneself to a morally sensitive theological position.

There is also another, formally different, possibility: suppose that instead of religious thinkers coming up with proposals that clash with those of Nhat Hahn, Chopra, and Spong but that still apparently solve the pluralist challenge, we imagine a situation in which the plausibility structure for my beliefs is propped up not by explicitly harmonizing my beliefs with those of potentially disconfirming Others but in a different fashion. I have argued elsewhere that it might be possible to construct a distinct spiritual community held together not by explicit agreement about the tenets of individual members' beliefs but by the commitment of the community or church to support each seeker's quest.[6] There would be common beliefs here too, but they would be on a different level; they would be beliefs about the dignity of all human beings and of their various spiritual quests. This approach too might be able to disarm the disconfirming power of the Other and provide a robust plausibility structure for each member's beliefs, but it would be operating on the level of attitudes of the community toward the general project of belief rather than on the level of particular theological convictions. It is an approach that seems well adapted to contemporary American sensibilities, with their egalitarian yearning to let as many persons as possible into the inner circle of spiritual life without sacrificing one's own most basic convictions. Yet, here too there is no necessary correlation between this program's ability to disarm the threatening aspects of pluralism and the truth of any of the beliefs embraced in any of the spiritual quests going on within the community.

Of course none of this implies that it is impossible to come up with arguments in addition to those we have been examining – we have been focused here specifically upon the challenge of the disconfirming Other – that would in fact provide evidence in favor of the existence of the divine or ultimate as our modification strategies perceive it. The point, however, is that this is a task that we have not even begun to undertake and which, while we cannot rule out its possible success, we have no way of knowing in advance can be successful. It is advisable to remember that Christian thinkers have for centuries attempted to come up with "proofs" for the existence of God, or at least with arguments that suggest the preponderance of evidence in theism's favor, and that they have been unable decisively to close that intellectually challenging deal. Of course, it may be easier to meet the age-old challenge of coming up with convincing evidence for the existence of the ultimate once the modification strategies have at least prevented the apparently different claims of the competing world religions from canceling one another out.

What, then, should be our penultimate conclusion about American religious and spiritual pluralism as a threat to belief? We can express that penultimate conclusion in the form of five brief propositions: First, pluralism does, without a doubt, raise the specter of the disconfirming Other. Second, it is possible to craft modification strategies that will render the religious Other friend rather than foe so that the disconfirmation challenge is met, with the moral bonus that one need no longer bear the guilt associated with looking down on religious Others. Third, there is no way of knowing, however, how many persons in American culture will be interested in and willing to embrace such modifications to their belief systems. An all-too-familiar American anti-intellectualism suggests that only a small percentage of believers will be interested in pursuing the project of faith seeking understanding with the sort of rigor that analysis and adoption of the modification strategies demand. Fourth, there are possible side-effects of taking up those modifications that suggest that religious and spiritual pluralism will, when all is said and done, still prove a threat to faith. Those side-effects include dislodging the believer from his or her erstwhile religious community, which may, in addition, lead him or her to view piety in terms of the New Age emphasis on technique and commodification, which tends to push the truth question out of the picture. Finally, if the modification strategies, whether or not they point one toward technique and commodification in one's spiritual life, have no implications for the truth of one's modified beliefs, then the all-important truth question will stand in its own way as a challenge to the modification strategies, as it has challenged more traditional views of the divine throughout modernity.

There is one more topic left to consider: the five conclusions just summarized are only penultimate because, in our investigation thus far, we have left out any analysis of the challenges that natural science poses to piety in the present day and age. This was no mere oversight. In Chapter One we observed, just in passing, that some commentators predict that the scientific worldview will eventually lead to a thoroughgoing secularization of even a culture as religiously and spiritually energetic as American culture. But our interest throughout this study has lain elsewhere, namely, with how spiritual and religious pluralism can threaten belief and with the different approach believers can take to this challenge. But we ought not wrap up our investigation without noting that, though it is usually not understood in this fashion in the perennial debate between science and religion, the scientific worldview can be viewed as one more voice in the pluralism that is at issue for us, one more instance of the potentially disconfirming Other.

At first blush, the notion of science as yet another form of the disconfirming Other because it is an additional belief system seems to result from a confusion. Suppose that we think of each of the belief systems of each of the great world religions as a circle. If the modification strategies can be trusted, then in terms of their specific truth claims, and especially where the general category of topics they address is concerned, these circles have large areas of overlap. That is, while some of the specific content of the religions differs, modification strategies or no, the aspects of life and the universe that each attempts to explain – we are keeping intact our focus upon the cognitive dimension – are much the same. For instance, each religion senses that human life is, as the Buddhists have put it, out of joint, and each religion has its analysis as to just what causes that problem. In addition, each of the religions supposes that the key to dealing with the slings and arrows that finitude thrusts our way is to move beyond the merely finite realm. Theists will see this goal in terms of proper relation to God; others will look to an impersonal infinite such as the Tao or an infinite state such as Nirvana.

Now natural science can hardly be one more circle massively overlapping these religious belief systems, for science ordinarily limits itself to empirical investigation of the physical world. An investigative procedure that, at least methodologically speaking, takes materialist reductionism as its vantage point upon reality can, strictly speaking, neither investigate realities that lie beyond matter-energy nor offer judgments about their reality or unreality. The mistake that has too often been made, however, when talking about religion or spirituality and science is to suppose that if science is indeed limited to the realm of matter-energy, it can have nothing to say about religious beliefs. But in fact science and spirituality do have points of contact. While there are large areas of the Christian worldview, for instance, that speak of matters wholly outside the purview of the scientific method, there are other portions of that Christian worldview that cannot avoid making assumptions about the universe of matter-energy that is science's area of expertise. For instance, if God is said to have miraculously cured someone of cancer, practitioners of science, while methodologically unable to view the divine cause, will of course be able to see the effect wrought by that cause. What is more, if they had sufficiently intricate tools to investigate that effect in perfect detail, they would notice a violation of the law of conservation of matter and energy.[7] God would have to have smuggled energy from outside the closed system of the physical universe into the inner workings of that universe. This would be the case even if God were to operate within the physical world by "pushing around" energy that already exists here: that "pushing" would itself require the extra, scientifically prohibited energy. In other words, a definite conflict arises here between spirituality and science; science and religion are not wholly separate arenas of discourse.

We can easily adduce other examples of spirituality and science both dealing with the physical universe in which we find ourselves, examples which suggest that science and religion are sometimes competing worldviews, each threatening the other with disconfirmation. Consider the notion that human beings possess an immaterial (and hence immortal) soul, a notion that most of the great world religions affirm in one way or another (even if the Buddha preached the doctrine of *anatman*, that is, "no self," he believed that there is something, if no more than a heap of qualities, that passes via spiritual inertia from one life to another and eventually into Nirvana). Those religions such as Christianity and Hinduism and Islam that put particular emphasis on the notion of a soul see it as distinguishable, if not wholly unconnected, from the physical dimensions of our being. At the same time, the Abrahamic religions most often think of the soul as the seat of our identities, the deep center within which our personalities are formed and which directly affects our behavior in the world, especially our moral behavior. But the materialist worldview of the neuroscientist suggests that the most distinguishing aspects of our personalities can be changed by changing the physical organ that is the human brain. Imbibing alcohol can turn a usually well-mannered man into the proverbial "mean drunk" who goes home from the bar and beats his wife and children. Or a stroke can take a person who had been unfailingly gracious and kind into a cantankerous curmudgeon who spends most of his or her time cursing and complaining. But surely these instances show that an object of science, the purely physical human brain, is the cause of who we are in a fashion that spiritualities have traditionally asserted could only be a function of an immaterial soul. Spirituality and science meet here, and that meeting seems to be a contentious one.

It is a notorious fact that, even in the present day and age, there are biblical literalists within the Christian community who hold that to embrace the Darwinian notion of evolution through natural selection would be to succumb to the disconfirmation of one's

THE MODIFICATION STRATEGIES   161

religious convictions. Although they have attempted strategically to appropriate different labels for the program that they want to advance – for instance, "creationism," "creation science," and, most recently, "intelligent design" theory – their goal is always the same, namely, to defend their biblical literalism at whatever points that literalism seems to be falsified by the natural sciences.

One response to the potential conflicts between spirituality and science is simply to embrace a willful ignorance about the scientific worldview and these potential conflicts with spirituality and religion. At first blush, this sort of avoidance technique seems formally similar to the sort of avoidance techniques we discussed in Chapter One, techniques that were intended to protect one's own beliefs from the challenge of the disconfirming Others who are devotees of other world religions. But upon closer inspection, we find an important difference between the two instances of avoidance: where the potentially disconfirming power of another world religion is concerned, we can avoid facing the threat of disconfirmation by trying to avoid thinking about the other religious traditions. One reason for the possible "success" of this avoidance maneuver is that, while there are persons of other faiths all around me in the United States, I do not actually participate in any of those other traditions. In our pluralistic society, I necessarily rub up against Buddhism and Islam, for example, but I may be able to put the implications of their existence out of my mind insofar as I have not accepted any of their unique tenets.

But surely the majority of Americans are in a different situation *vis-à-vis* the scientific worldview. While we may refuse to believe in particular results of that worldview such as biological evolution, we happily embrace other components of the scientific worldview, whether we wish to or not, in a host of circumstances. For instance, we are convinced that antibiotics can oftentimes eliminate infections from which we suffer. And consider that most all of us would be furious if, while suffering the symptoms of a heart attack, we were rushed to a hospital where the staff responded by chanting, dancing, and burning incense rather than with medical interventions grounded in the scientific worldview.

Thus it is that we find ourselves with a new version of the problem of fragilization represented by pluralism. There is a plurality of spiritual and religious worldviews, but in addition to all of these there is another worldview that the vast majority of Americans at least tacitly embrace, namely the scientific worldview – Sallie McFague goes so far as to call scientific accounts of our origin the "common creation story"[8] – and it sometimes contradicts spiritual convictions to a sufficient degree that it counts as another version of the potentially disconfirming power of pluralism. Of course, unlike the case of the disconfirming threats represented by world religions confronting one another, the pluralism represented by a religious worldview confronted with the scientific worldview is that *this* pluralism and its concomitant conflict tends to exist *within* the mind of a single individual.

What, then, are the implications of this science-centered variation on the theme of the disconfirming Other? Perhaps some fine-tuning of the modification strategies that we have explicated in Chapters Three and Four might be able to equip them to deal with this new, scientific player in our story about spirituality and pluralism. But there is another possibility as well. In briefly treating the modification strategies' irrelevance to the truth question above, we noted the very real possibility that one could construct alternative modification strategies, strategies concentrating on themes other than immanence, experience, and ineffability. Perhaps the challenge of the scientific worldview to some forms of spirituality and religion can best be met by making harmony with science the guiding principle in constructing a modification strategy, and only when that is achieved moving on to mold the strategies so that they can avoid the mutual fragilization of spiritual perspectives that has been our concern in this study. But that is, as the saying goes, another story for another time.[9]

Notes

Introduction

   1. Charles Taylor, *A Secular Age* (Cambridge: Harvard University Press, 2007), p. 303. In the latter half of the twentieth century, "the Other" became a familiar expression, especially among thinkers loosely allied under the label "postmodernism." In that case, "the Other" often referred to persons who are politically, economically, and socially marginalized. The Other is not only regarded as threatening and alien, but as a necessary foil for those possessing power, someone over whom they can exercise their power and privilege. This reading of the Other was given particular saliency by the French philosopher Alexandre Kojéve in his lectures on G.W.F. Hegel's interpretation of the relationship between master and slave. All of this might well be relevant to my coming face to face with the religious Other. However, the emphasis in what follows is focused upon my ability to maintain the intellectual integrity of my religious beliefs in the face of very different beliefs; the Other is primarily an intellectual, cognitive threat here.

   2. I shall be referring frequently in this study to the notion of a social plausibility structure for religious belief, a notion that I borrow from Peter Berger's classic book, *The Sacred Canopy: Elements of a Sociological Theory of Religion* (Garden City, NY: Doubleday/Anchor Books, 1967).

   3. Orthodox, Conservative, and Reform Judaism can each be taken as "mainline" examples of American Judaism despite the differences in belief and practice among them. Christianity faces a larger challenge from the sort of pluralism we will be examining because of Christianity's greater traditional emphasis upon doctrine and theology.

4. See Catherine L. Albanese, *A Republic of Mind and Spirit: A Cultural History of American Metaphysical Religion* (New Haven: Yale University Press, 2007).

5. Winthrop S. Hudson and John Corrigan, *Religion in America*, fifth edition (New York: Macmillan, 1992), p. 34.

6. Hudson and Corrigan, *Religion in America*, p. 57.

7. As anyone familiar with the academic study of religion as it has been carried out in the past few decades is well aware, the attempt to define religion, indeed even the notion that there exists a discrete phenomenon corresponding to the term "religion," has been much debated. While I shall make reference to the "return of religion" in my comments on secularization below and will address the challenges in defining religion at the end of Chapter Three, it is important to note that here at the outset I have self-consciously stipulated working definitions for both "religion" and "spirituality." This will allow us to focus upon particular phenomena without advancing the claim that there is some objective essence of religion and of spirituality that is, in each case, independent of our interpretive prejudices and simply waiting for us to discover it.

Given the stipulative definitions that I have provided, the title of this book might more accurately be rendered as "*Spiritual* Pluralism as a Threat to Belief," since spiritual pluralism is the broader category and since non-institutional forms of piety embraced by the Other could in principle be as disconfirming as institutional, "religious" ones. But due to the potentially unfamiliar character of my stipulative definitions and to the fact that the expression "spiritual pluralism" is much less familiar than "religious pluralism," I have chosen the latter formulation for the book's title.

8. See Garry Wills, *Head and Heart: American Christianities* (New York: Penguin, 2007), p. 7.

9. See, for example, David D. Hall, *Worlds of Wonder, Days of Judgment: Popular Religious Belief in Early New England* (Cambridge: Harvard University Press, 1990). It must be acknowledged, of course, that some of folk piety's investment in supernatural interventions in the natural order were brought into the orbit of more mainstream Christian thinking by attributing such interventions to God and the devil. The same cannot be said, however, for something such as astrology.

10. Quoted in Jaroslav Pelikan, *Jesus Through the Centuries: His Place in the History of Culture* (New Haven: Yale University Press, 1999), p. 97.

11. See Søren Kierkegaard, *Fear and Trembling; Repetition*, trans. Howard V. Hong (Princeton: Princeton University Press, 1983).

12. Andrew Greeley and Michael Hout, *The Truth About Conservative Christians: What They Think and What They Believe* (Chicago: University of Chicago: 2006), p. 14.

13. Albanese, *A Republic of Mind and Spirit*, p. 13. Further references to this source in this chapter will be cited in the text by page number only.

14. As we have defined "religion" and "spirituality," the latter's susceptibility to secularization might be conceived as significantly less than religion's. Secularization is often defined in terms of piety's retreat from the centers of power in the larger society to the private sphere. Given that spirituality is at home in the private sphere, this version of secularization, at least, is much more corrosive of religion than of spirituality. This has, in fact, been one argument against secularization theory. It often suggests that piety in general is being continually weakened when in fact piety is as strong as ever: it is simply that institutional forms of piety are being exchanged for more private ones. However, in countries such as Sweden and Denmark, even private spiritual convictions seem to have largely disappeared from among the populace. See Phil Zuckerman, *Society without God: What the Least Religious Nations Can Tell Us about Contentment* (New York: New York University Press, 2008).

15. Gregory S. Paul, "The Big Religion Questions Finally Solved," *Free Inquiry,* December 2008/January 2009: 28.

16. Paul, "The Big Questions Finally Solved," p. 28.

17. "U.S. Religious Landscape Survey 2008, Washington, D.C.: The Pew Forum on Religion and Public Life, 2008.

18. "U.S. Religious Landscape Survey," p. 5.

19. "U.S. Religious Landscape Survey," p. 5.

20. See Greeley and Hout, *The Truth About Conservative Christians*, p. 7.

21. "U.S. Religious Landscape Survey," p. 7.

22. John L. Esposito and Dalia Mogahed, eds., *Who Speaks for Islam? What a Billion Muslims Really Think* (New York: Gallup Press, 2007), p. 6.

23. Jon Meacham, "The Decline and Fall of Christian America," *Newsweek*, April 13, 2009, 34-38. Meacham's article is the cover story, and that cover, with its title displayed in bright red letters against a black background, cleverly alludes to *Time*'s notorious April 8, 1966 cover which boldly asked, in large red letters on a pure black background, "Is God Dead?" The latter was a reference to the "death of God theology" then much in vogue in some circles. Further references to this source will be cited in the text of my essay by page number only.

24. David Ramsey Steele, "Is God Coming Or Going?," *Philosophy Now*, April/May 2010: 10.

25. Lewis Black, *Me of Little Faith*, ed. Hank Gallo (New York: Riverhead Books, 2008), p. 4.

26. Black, *Me of Little Faith*, p. 182.

27. Black, *Me of Little Faith*, p. 35.

Chapter One

1. John Locke, "Essay Concerning Human Understanding," in *Eighteenth-Century Philosophy*, ed. Lewis White Beck (New York: Free Press, 1966), p. 57.

2. *Dei Filius*, in *Documents of Vatican Council I*, trans. John Broderick (Collegeville, Minnesota: Liturgical Press, 1971), p. 43. (italics mine)

3. See Søren Kierkegaard, *Fear and Trembling*, in Søren Kierkegaard, *Fear and Trembling and The Sickness Unto Death*, trans Walter Lowrie (Princeton: Princeton University Press, 1974).

4. See Mircea Eliade, *The Sacred and the Profane: The Nature of Religion*, trans. Willard R. Trask (New York: Harcourt, Brace, and World, 1959),

5. See Richard Dawkins, *The God Delusion* (Boston: Houghton Mifflin, 2006), and Sam Harris, *The End of Faith: Religion, Terror, and the Future of Reason* (New York: Norton, 2004).

6. It must be acknowledged, of course, that while there is, at present, something approaching a common, secular American morality focusing on family values, there are sub-issues under the general heading of family values – abortion comes to mind as an example – that frequently collide with a particular perception of the sacred. Yet what so upsets the anti-abortionist is the fact that abortion is still legal in this country, which suggests to the abortion opponent precisely that the secular component of American culture is almost entirely independent of what he or she takes to be the demands of the sacred.

7. Rita Carter, *Multiplicity: The New Science of Personality, Identity, and the Self* (New York: Little, Brown, 2008), p. 20 (ellipsis in original).

8. Carter, *Multiplicity*, p. 20.

9. Carter actually uses the word "compartmentalization" as a technical term denoting one particular manner in which the brain can produce a multi-faceted self. By contrast, I am utilizing the term in the broader sense of the ability to hold contradictory notions by keeping those notions in temporally separate compartments. The overall thesis of Carter's book is that, while what psychiatrists call Multiple Personality Disorder is indeed an extreme condition that must be deemed pathological, even the best-adjusted person is characterized not by a single, discrete personality, but,

rather, by an array of loosely allied sub-personalities. For her technical use of "compartmentalization," see *Multiplicity*, pp. 67-69.

10. Carter, *Multiplicity*, p. 21.

11. See, for example, Paul Tillich, *Dynamics of Faith* (New York: Perennial, 2001), 1-4.

12. Georges Roy, "Meta-atheism: Religious Avowal as Self-Deception," in Louise M. Antony, ed., *Philosophers Without God: Meditations on Atheism and the Secular Life* (New York: Oxford Press, 2007), p. 245.

13. Roy, "Meta-atheism," p. 252.

14. Michael S. Gazzaniga, *Human: The Science Behind What Makes Us Unique* (New York: HarperCollins, 2000), p. 102.

15. Sigmund Freud, *The Future of an Illusion*, trans. James Strachey (New York: W.W. Norton, 1961).

16. Dorothy Rowe, "Tell Me Lies, Tell Me Sweet Little Lies . . ." *New Scientist*, June 19-25, 2010: 29.

Chapter Two

1. Randall Balmer, *Mine Eyes Have Seen the Glory: A Journey into the Evangelical Subculture in America*, third edition (New York: Oxford University Press, 2000), p. 95.

2. Balmer, *Mine Eyes Have Seen the Glory*, p. 133.

3. Reverend Bailey Smith, http://www.time.com/time/magazine/article/0,9171,9528100.00/html. Accessed January 16, 2010.

4. "Conservative Christians," in Greeley and Hout's sense, are defined by being inheritors of the principles of the Protestant Reformation; by belonging to particular denominations; by embracing biblical literalism, the born-again experience, and the duty to evangelize; and by tending to hold what are usually classified as conservative political positions. Given this last characteristic, "Conservative Christians" are to be distinguished from members of African-American denominations, whose members may share the other characteristics listed here. See Greeley and Hout, *The Truth About Conservative Christians*.

5. Of course, this requires that the fundamentalist does not allow himself or herself actually to confront the disconfirming logic represented by spiritual pluralism.

6. Tim F. LeHaye and Jerry B. Jenkins, *Left Behind* (Wheaton, Illinois: Tyndale, 1998). This is the first installment in what turned out to be a series of sixteen books, with the last published in 2007. The film version (2001) was produced by Cloud Ten Pictures in association with Namesake Entertainment and directed by Vic Sarin.

7. See Malise Ruthven, *Fundamentalism: The Search for Meaning* (New York: Oxford University Press, 2004), p. 11.

8. "Speaker at McCain rally says non-Christians want an Obama win," www.cnn.com, October 12, 2008. The rally was held on October 11, 2008.

9. Balmer, *Mine Eyes Have Seen the Glory,* p. 133.

10. That evasion is a part of the fundamentalist use of the sense of moral responsibility to trump the disconfirming power of pluralism is pointed out in note 5 above.

11. We ought not to forget, however, that fundamentalism is, in its own way, a modification of traditional Christian belief rather than the simple defense of that belief that it claims to be. As we have seen, Christian fundamentalism is a peculiarly modern phenomenon, a movement that picks as fundamental precisely those beliefs that appear to be under attack in the modern and contemporary worlds. It is instructive, for instance, that Biblical inerrancy was not taught by Martin Luther in the fashion that it is by Christian fundamentalists.

Chapter Three

1. Gustav Niebuhr, *Beyond Tolerance: Searching for Interfaith Understanding in America* (New York: Viking Press, 2008), p. xvi.

2. Quoted in Niebuhr, *Beyond Tolerance*, p. xxiv.

3. For a helpful analysis of the present state of the discussion of exclusivism, inclusivism, and pluralism, see Hugh Nicholson, "The Reunification of Theology and Comparison in the New Comparative Theology," *Journal of the American Academy of Religion* (September 2009): 609-46.

4. It is important to understand at the outset of this chapter that neither it, nor this book as a whole, is intended as an effort to construct a pluralist theology or a "theology of religions." First of all, I undertake no foundational work exploring the notion of the ultimate, work that is usually necessary for a pluralist theology (we need to know something about the ultimate in order to explain how it can be the object of multiple religions). More important, nothing in this chapter or the chapters that follow endorses a particular form of pluralist theology. Rather, the goal is to explore the contemporary cultural appeal of understanding the world religions as compatible, particularly in the light of the challenge of the disconfirming Other. And while our point of entry into this topic does make mention of John Hick's famous pluralist theology, the heart of our endeavor deals with three popular writers (only one of whom is a Christian). None of them attempts to build a full-scale "world theology" or "theology of religions":

Thich Nhat Hahn and Deepak Chopra try to show the compatibility of Christianity with their own Asian spiritual sensibilities. Bishop Shelby Spong mentions compatibility only in passing but sets forth a theological proposal that jells in relevant respects with what the other two writers have to say. Finally, I make no truth claims about the modification strategies that I find in the books by Nhat Hahn, Chopra, and Spong. In short, the goal of this study is not to advocate a new world theology, but, rather, to explore the problem of the disconfirming Other and how contemporary sensibilities align in such a way as to favor a particular type of modification strategies. This exploration will include a consideration of the potential pitfalls of the kind of modification strategies under review.

5. For the best overview of the material in Rahner's thought that is of interest to us, see his *Foundations of Christian Faith: An Introduction to the Idea of Christianity*, trans. William V. Dych (New York: Seabury Press, 1978).

6. Joseph Ratzinger, *What It Means to Be a Christian: Three Sermons*, trans. Henry Taylor (San Francisco: Ignatius Press, 2005), p. 45.

7. Ratzinger, *What It Means to be a Christian*, p. 46. Lest there be any confusion on the matter, it should be emphasized that Pope Benedict opposes, in no uncertain terms, a full-blown pluralist theology, in which Jesus Christ's unique role in humanity's salvation would be relativized. See especially his Declaration "*Dominus Iesus*: On the Unicity and Salvific Univerality of Jesus Christ and the Church," issued when Benedict, as Cardinal Ratzinger, was head of the Church's Congregation for for the Doctrine of the Faith (often described as Roman Catholicism's "doctrinal watchdog" agency). The Declaration is available at the Vatican website, www.vatican.va. See also Joseph Cardinal Ratzinger, *Truth and Tolerance: Christian Belief and World Religions*, trans. Henry Taylor (San Francisco: Ignatius Press, 2004).

8. See John Hick, *Philosophy of Religion*, 4th ed. (Upper Saddle River, New Jersey: Prentice-Hall, 1990), pp. 112-19.

9. As I have attempted consistently to make clear, given the many strata that constitute spiritual and religious phenomena, there are also myriad ways to study those phenomena, and in this book I am concentrating on the portions amenable to theology and philosophy of religion. But even the specific question at issue for us here, namely, pluralism and how believers' attitudes to it may change over time, can be studied with tools such as socio-economic analysis and game-theory, as is made evident by Robert Wright in his book *The Evolution of God* (New York: Little, Brown: 2009). Wright makes much of the notion of "non-zero-sum" games or situations versus a "zero-sum" scenario. The latter is

illustrated by you and I making a bet for five dollars. If you win, I have to pay you five dollars: a five-dollar bill leaves my wallet, never to return, while your wallet acquires a new bill. One person must always end up with a score of zero. But other games and phenomena are non-zero sum undertakings. They are "win-win." We see the non-zero-sum dynamic at work, argues Wright, when members of two different groups recognize that cooperation with the other group will be of advantage to them both (as often happens, for example, as the world economy evolves). Wright sees this in spirituality too, so that it is almost inevitable that spiritual or religious groups will move from something akin to exclusivism to something more like what, on the theological level, we are calling pluralist thinking about the divine.

10. See, for example, Alvin Plantinga, "Reason and Belief in God," in *Faith and Rationality*, ed. Alvin Plantinga and Nicholas Wolterstorff (South Bend, Indiana: University of Notre Dame Press, 1983), pp. 16-93.

11. George A. Lindbeck, *The Nature of Doctrine: Religion and Theology in a Postliberal Age* (Philadelphia: Westminster Press, 1984).

12. Lindbeck, *The Nature of Doctrine*, p. 49.

13. It is worth nothing that, for Lindbeck, some Christian language, specifically what are usually labeled "doctrines," are, contrary to initial appearances, not propositions at all, and hence cannot be threatened by the propositions found in others' belief systems. Rather, doctrines are second-order rules that specify how first-order propositions are to be properly used. What Lindbeck fails to acknowledge, however, as I read him, is that doctrines such as the pronouncements of the Council of Nicea about Jesus being of the same substance as the Father, *presuppose* various first-order propositions about God and the Christian life. He does point out that doctrines rest upon *some* first-order propositions, but he does not include God-talk itself among these propositions. Lindbeck's interest in doctrines in particular is a function of the central concern of his book, namely, the ecumenical dialogue within Christianity.

14. Lindbeck, *The Nature of Doctrine*, p. 51.

15. Lindbeck, *The Nature of Doctrine*, p. 50.

16. When Lindbeck's book appeared in 1984, the cultural-linguistic approach to studying religions had, as he himself points out, already made significant inroads in various academic circles, but not in Christian theology, the reflection on Christian faith carried out from the perspective of that faith itself. There was, then, something undeniably refreshing and provocative about Lindbeck's application of the cultural-linguistic perspective within the discipline of theology. Time has marched on,

however, and the cultural-linguistic approach in general, particularly insofar as it is considered a form of postmodernist or post-structuralist theory, has lost ground as it has been attacked by those embracing other perspectives, including cognitive science, which puts much greater emphasis upon common human traits, traits built into the human brain, than the cultural-linguistic school allows. As an example of such an attack, one concerned with understanding religion in particular, see D. Jason Slone, *Theological Incorrectness: Why Religious People Believe What They Shouldn't* (New York: Oxford University Press, 2004). We shall return to Lindbeck's reflections on religion, this time to consider his contrast between the cultural-linguistic approach and what he calls "experiential-expressivism," in Chapter Four below.

17. While both Plantinga and Lindbeck are motivated by relatively orthodox Christian convictions, James Carse provides a more radical approach to thinking about Christianity and the other world religions, but it too might be taken to erase the apparent problem of pluralism and the disconfirming Other: Carse holds that religion is not about belief at all! While Carse's position is genuinely intriguing, it seems to me that Carse's approach cannot help us avoid disconfirmation by the Other, for the simple reason that the vast majority of the adherents of the world religions do suppose that religion entails belief. See James P. Carse, *The Religious Case Against Belief* (New York: Penguin, 2008).

18. Thich Nhat Hanh, *Living Buddha, Living Christ* (New York: Riverhead, 1995), p.1. Further quotations from this book will be cited by page number in the body of my essay.

19. Deepak Chopra, *The Third Jesus: The Christ We Cannot Ignore* (New York: Harmony Books, 2008), p. 211. Further quotations from this book will be cited by page number in the body of my essay.

20. Schleiermacher's central exploration of God-consciousness is to be found in his *The Christian Faith*, trans. and ed. H.R. Mackintosh and J.S. Stewart (Philadelphia: Fortress Press, 1976).

21. Oddly enough, the one place where Chopra's broad-minded pluralist approach displays a dismaying lacuna is in his references to Judaism. He takes for granted the old Christian portrayal of the Judaism of Jesus' day as an unimaginative, constrictive legalism and projects upon that Judaism the distinctively Christian doctrine of original sin. See, for example, *The Third Jesus*, p. 17. One wonders whether, in addition to a simple lack of historical knowledge of Judaism, Chopra's misapprehensions are fueled by his special reliance on the notoriously anti-Jewish Gospel of John for his interpretation of Jesus.

22. Regarding Chopra's apparently more quietest take thanks to his notion of the everyday world as one of illusion, see, for example, *The Third Jesus*: "physical life, even at its most cruel, can be transcended" (i.e., in consciousness) (p. 111). In a similar fashion, he also says: "The rescue that people need today won't conquer Caesar [Jesus' designation for the political powers that be], but it will conquer duality. Jesus symbolized the transcendent self that renders the ego irrelevant and transforms duality into oneness with God" (p. 217).

23. John Shelby Spong, *Jesus for the Non-Religious: Recovering the Divine at the Heart of the Human* (San Francisco: HarperSanFrancisco, 2007), p. 222. Further quotations from this book will be cited by page number in the body of my essay.

24. If we juxtapose the material elements at the heart of this modification strategy – the emphases on immanence, experience, and ineffability – with the formal approach that our ideal type of Christian (described in the Introduction) takes toward belief, an approach that privileges the cognitive dimension of spirituality, it is tempting to see a tension. If I am particularly invested in the cognitive dimensions of the Christian life, and if it is precisely that focus on the cognitive that attunes me to the disconfirming power of the Other and disposes me toward the modification strategy exemplified by Nhat Hahn, Chopra, and Spong, what are we to make of the fact that that modification strategy itself edges away from cognition and toward experience and ineffability? The answer is to be found in the distinction between the formal and material sides of the equation made above: there is no tension or contradiction, for my cognitive focus is what allows me to calculate and to understand that movement toward a greater emphasis on experience and ineffability will negate the Other's ability to effect disconfirmation.

25. Quoted in Mark C. Taylor, *After God* (Chicago: University of Chicago Press, 2007), p. 5.

26. We have drawn upon Eliade at some length above. For Otto's central work, see *The Idea of the Holy: An Inquiry into the Non-Rational Factor in the Idea of the Divine and Its Relation to the Rational*, trans. John W. Harvey (New York: Oxford University Press, 1958).

27. *Catechism of the Catholic Church* (New Hope Kentucky: Urbi et Orbi, 1994), pp. 115-16; emphasis in original.

28. Karl Menninger, *Whatever Became of Sin?* (New York: Hawthorn, Press, 1973).

29. Anselm, *Cur Deus Homo?*, trans. Sidney Norton Deane (Chicago: Open Court Press, 1903).

Chapter Four

1. See, for example, Mircea Eliade, ed., *Essential Sacred Writings from Around the World* (San Francisco: HarperSanFrancisco, 1967), pp. 5-7.

2. Peter Berger explains Weber's perspective in *The Sacred Canopy: Elements of a Sociological Theory of Religion* (Garden City, New York: Doubleday/Anchor Books, 1967), p. 111.

3. The forms of Protestantism that are least likely to disenchant the world may well be those rooted in Pietism, for that tradition often views the relationship of the individual believer with Jesus Christ not as threatening and distant, but as personal and akin to the friendship between two human beings. Some commentators go so far as to suggest an erotic relationship in Pietism between Jesus and the believer.

4. Mark C. Taylor, *After God*, p. 297. Taylor's observation here is more applicable to the history of modern Protestant theology than to Roman Catholic thought.

5. See, for example, David Tracy, *Blessed Rage for Order: The New Pluralism in Theology* (New York: Seabury, 1975), and Sallie McFague, *Metaphorical Theology: Models of God in Religious Language* (Philadelphia: Fortress Press, 1982).

6. See Mark C. Taylor, *Erring: A Postmodern A/Theology* (Chicago: University of Chicago Press, 1984).

7. See Rosemary Radford Ruether, *Sexism and God-Talk: Toward a Feminist Theology* (Boston: Beacon, 1983).

8. Harold Bloom, *The American Religion: The Emergence of the Post-Christian Nation* (New York: Simon and Schuster, 1992).

9. Thich Nhat Hahan, *Living Buddha, Living Christ*, p. 194.

10. Immanuel Kant, *Critique of Pure Reason*, trans. Norman Kemp Smith (New York: St. Martin's Press, 1965), p. 171.

11. One might object that the sort of experience generated with the help of sensible intuition is already "internal experience," given that it too – indeed any sort of experience, qua experience – plays itself out in the mind (and is powerfully molded by the mind, if one accepts the whole of Kant's philosophy). But it is evident, I think, that what we are designating "internal experience" has a peculiar right to that designation insofar as it plays itself out in the mind without being (directly) dependent upon sensible intuition, which can be traced back to physical phenomena external to the mind. Of course, the God believed to be given to consciousness via this internal experience is claimed to be external to the mind as well, but not in the manner of a physical object; God's externality

to the mind is not one of physical distance. What is more, as we have emphasized, this God can be claimed to be immanent at the same time that it is external or transcendent to the mind.

12. Lindbeck, *The Nature of Doctrine*, p. 21.

13. Lindbeck, *The Nature of Doctrine,* p. 31.

14. For a particularly perceptive account of Buddhism's role in contemporary America, see Chapter Twelve, "Western *Dharmas*," in Pankaj Mishra, *An End to Suffering: The Buddha in the World* (New York: Picador Press, 2004).

15. *The Holy Qur'an*, text, translation, and commentary by A. Yusuf Ali (Brentwood, Maryland: Amana Press, 1983).

16. See Hick, *Philosophy of Religion*, p. 115.

17. Of course, we have produced no arguments showing that the divine or infinite actually is immanent within human consciousness, nor that the divine can be and actually is experienced by some spiritually inclined persons, nor that such experience and its object, if they exist, are necessarily in some sense ineffable. All we have is the testimony of Nhat Hahn, Chopra, and Spong. Thus, our investigation should in no way be confused with a foundational or apologetic theology: the reality of the ultimate that the believer wants to protect from disconfirmation by the Other may or may not exist. Our concern, rather, has simply been to show how certain modification strategies can render the Other's beliefs consistent with the believer's own and thus no longer disconfirming. Whether the beliefs in question are "true," whether they accurately reflect reality, has not been and will not be part of our topic.

Chapter Five

1. See above, p. 9.

2. See the "Coda" in Albanese, *A Republic of Mind and Spirit*.

3. At least they need not conflict when viewed simply as practices. If, however, we insist that all such practices presuppose facts about the world and the way in which it works, which indeed they do, then we may reasonably look for contradictions also among the conceptual underpinnings of diverse practices. It is simply that the majority of New Age teachers – though not all, as we shall see below in our discussion of those who attempt to enlist science on behalf of the New Age – have effected an epistemic reordering such that the ontological claims about how the universe is ultimately put together (claims that are on the top rung of our ideal Christian's spiritual concerns, claims that deal with the reality

of God, after all) are now relegated to a lower rung of the ladder, with the top rung now occupied with subjective perceptions of therapeutic efficacy.

4. See, for example, Michael Shermer, "Hope Springs Eternal: Science, the Afterlife, and The Meaning of Life," *The Skeptic*, 13, no. 4 (2010): 52-55, and Michael Shermer, *How We Believe: Science, Skepticism, and the Search for God*, 2nd ed. (New York: Henry Holt, 2003), pp. 48-58. Shermer actually critiques John Edward and James Van Praagh in particular.

5. For a particularly thorough exercise in the scientific scrutiny of alternative medicine, see R. Barker Bausell, *Snake Oil Science: The Truth about Complementary and Alternative Medicine* (New York: Oxford University Press, 2007).

6. Susan Blackmore, "Where Are You, Sue?" in *What Have You Changed Your Mind About: Today's Leading Minds Rethink Everything*, ed. John Brockman (New York: HarperCollins, 2009), p. 19.

7. Blackmore, "Where Are You, Sue?," p. 20.

8. See, as but one example, Benedict Carey, "Long-Awaited Medical Study Questions the Power of Prayer," *New York Times*, March 31, 2006, p. 1.

9. Lynne McTaggart, *The Field: The Quest for the Secret Force of the Universe*, updated ed. (New York: Harper, 2008), p. *xxiii*.

10. Phaedra and Isaac Bonewits, *Real Energy: Systems, Spirits, and Substances to Heal, Change, and Grow* (Franklin Lakes, NJ: Career Press, 2007).

11. See Victor J. Stenger, *Quantum Gods: Creation, Chaos, and the Search for Cosmic Consciousness* (Amherst, NY: Prometheus Books, 2009).

12. See Rhonda Byrne, *The Secret* (New York: Atria, 2006), and the film *What the Bleep Do We Know?* (2004), directed by Betsy Chasse *et al.*

13. See Michael Shermer, "Quantum Flapdoodle and Other Flummery," his Foreword to Victor Stenger's *Quantum Gods*, p. 8. Some readers, having seen the New Age's traditional emphasis on technique, and noting that even when New Agers give more weight than usual to the New Age as a belief system it remains inconsistent with the scientific worldview, might conclude that the New Age ought to be categorized not as "religion" but as "magic." The traditional divide between religion and magic suggests that, for the religious person, any supernatural favors granted one are the gracious gifts of a power beyond one's control, while magic is all about mastering techniques for controlling the world. Given that the religion versus magic distinction is most often invoked by those in favor of religion, it is not surprising that, despite the admiration, or even envy, that one might feel for Harry Potter, magic is usually frowned upon as a self-deceived quest for the essentially selfish ability to manipulate reality. However, given

that our approach to the New Age sees it as a contemporary manifestation of what Albanese calls metaphysical religion and that our particular concern is with its highly pluralistic character, it would not, I think, prove illuminating for us to pursue the magic versus religion distinction here.

Chapter Six

1. "Christians and Lions," *The Economist* (December 31, 2011-January 6, 2012): 9.

2. See Andrew Newberg, Eugene D'Aquili, and Vince Rause, *Why God Won't Go Away: Brain Science and the Biology of Belief* (New York: Ballantine Books, 2001), and Andrew Newberg and Mark Robert Waldman, *Born to Believe: God, Science, and the Origin of Ordinary and Extraordinary Beliefs* (New York: Free Press, 2006).

3. This goes to show that the plausibility structure for my belief being strengthened via the modifications has at least two different moments. First, and most important, the plausibility of my beliefs will be reinforced when I adopt the modifications. Second, the attractiveness and apparent wisdom of that process of adoption will itself seem the more plausible the larger the number of persons in my society who have already adopted the modifications before me.

4. See Paul Tillich, *Systematic Theology*, 3 vols. (Chicago: University of Chicago, 1951-63) vol. 2.

5. "Pew Forum: Many Americans Mix Multiple Faiths," at http://pewforum.org/docs/?DocID=490, p. 2. Accessed December 14, 2009.

6. For my attempt to treat this hypothesis in detail, see *To Re-Enchant the World: A Philosophy of Unitarian Universalism* (New York: Xlibris Press, 2004).

7. The first law of thermodynamics states that matter and energy in a closed system can never be either created or destroyed but can only change their form.

8. See Sallie McFague, *The Body of God: An Ecological Theology* (Minneapolis: Augsburg Fortress Press, 1993).

9. For an analysis that focuses exclusively upon making spiritual affirmations consistent with the scientific worldview, see my *Beyond the God Delusion: How Radical Theology Harmonizes Science and Religion* (Minneapolis: Fortress Press, 2008).

Index

Coleridge, Samuel Taylor, 7
Christian Science (Church of
  Jesus Christ Scientist), 9, 113
compartmentalization, of
  beliefs, 25, 37-38, 134,
  166n.9
Conrad, Arnold, 54
Corrigan, John, 4
Creedence Clearwater Revival, 7

Darwin, Charles, 38, 160-61
Dawkins, Richard, 34
Descartes, René, 111
Dei filius, 27
Dogma (film), 19

Edward, John, 136-37, 175n.4
Eliade, Mircea, 31, 33, 98
Eliot, T.S., 23
Ellison, Ralph, 112
Emerson, Ralph Waldo, 7, 112,
  125-26
Esposito, John, 165n.22
Eucharist, 84
exclusivism, 61, 168n.3
experience, religious, 81, 83,
  85, 86, 88, 89, 93-97, 108,
  113-29, 132, 151, 156, 162,
  172n.24, 173n.11

Falwell, Jerry, 56
fideism, 24-25, 28-29, 35, 40
Finke, Roger, 13
Freud, Sigmund, 42, 93, 112

Gallup Poll, 16, 17
Gazzaniga, Michael, 41, 43
Gell Mann, Murray, 141
Gorski, Philip S., 13

Greeley, Andrew, 8, 15, 46, 47,
  48, 167n.4
Grigg, Richard, 176n.6, 177n.9
ground of being, 85, 91, 96,
  115, 119

Hall, David D., 164n.9
Harris, Sam, 34
Hegel, G.W.F., 7, 163n.1
Heidegger, Martin, 112
Hick, John, 69-72, 83, 108,
  121, 122-24, 146, 168n.4
Hout, Michael, 8, 15, 46, 47,
  48, 167n.4
Hudson, Winthrop, 4

immanence, 81, 84, 92-3, 94,
  97, 108-13, 116, 121-27,
  128-29, 151, 156, 162,
  172n.24
inclusivism, 61, 62, 65, 69,
  121, 147, 168n.3
ineffability, 83, 93, 95, 96-97,
  108, 117-20, 121-25, 128-
  29, 151, 156, 162, 172n.24
Inglehart, Ronald, 17
intuition, 2, 88, 115-17, 123,
  146-49
Ives, Charles, 7

Jacobi, F.H., 7
Jaspers, Karl, 69, 122
Jenkins, Jerry B., 53
Jesus Christ, 2, 8, 10, 18, 27,
  31, 34, 36, 37, 45, 47, 48,
  52, 61, 64-65, 68, 71, 72,
  75, 81, 83-85, 87-97, 100,
  102, 103, 104, 106, 108,
  109-10, 119-20, 121, 126,

Jesus Christ (*cont.*)
127, 128, 152, 153, 155,
170n.13, 171n.21, 172n.22,
173n.3
John of the Cross, 117
Julian of Norwich, 117

Kant, Immanuel, 62, 69, 72,
111, 114, 173n.11
Karlstadt, Andreas, 126
Kierkegaard, Søren, 7, 29
King, Martin Luther, Jr.
Kojève, Alexandre, 163n.1
Krishna, 127

Left Behind (film), 53
LeHaye, Tim F., 53
Life of Brian (film), 19
Lindbeck, Geoge, 77-80, 116-
17, 118, 170n.13, 171n.16,
171n.17
Locke, John, 26-27, 29
Luther, Martin, 40, 126,
168n.11

Macbeth, 23
McCain, John, 54
McFague, Sallie, 111, 162
Mogahed, Dalia, 165n.22
McTaggart, Lynne, 140
Maher, Bill, 18
Marx, Karl, 12
Meachum, John, 17
Mencken, H.L., 17
Menninger, Karl, 103
Merton, Thomas, 80
Mishra, Pankaj, 174n.14
Möhler, Johann Adam, 111
Muhammad, 26, 90

Nhat Hahn, Thich, 23, 80-86,
88, 91, 92, 94, 96, 97, 101-
06, 108, 113, 115, 116, 119,
121, 123, 124, 125, 127,
128, 129, 147, 155, 156,
168n.4, 172n.24, 174n.17
Newberg, Andrew, 148-49
Newsweek Religion Survey, 17
Niebuhr, Gustav, 60
Nicholson, Hugh, 168n.3
Nietzsche, Friedrich, 78-93
Norris, Pippa, 17

Obama, Barack, 54
Oh God (film), 18-19
Otto, Rudolf, 98

Paul, Gregory, 13
Paul, Saint, 119
Pew Forum on Religion and
Public Life, 15, 16, 154-55
Plantinga, Alvin, 75-77, 79-80,
171n.17
Plato, 30-31
plausibility structure, 2, 55-58,
128-129, 146, 149, 150,
156, 163n.1, 176n.3
pluralist theology, 61, 63-64, 69,
70, 71, 80, 90, 121, 145-47,
155, 168n.3, 168n.4, 169n.9
proof,
of truth of religious belief,
22-23, 157,
and evidence, 74-80,
and lack of, regarding New
Age beliefs, 136-41

Rahner, Karl, 62-68, 69, 108,
121-22, 128, 145, 146-47